The Story of Arturo Toscanini

By DAVID EWEN in this same series

THE STORY OF IRVING BERLIN

THE STORY OF GEORGE GERSHWIN

TALES FROM THE VIENNA WOODS:
The Story of Johann Strauss

HAYDN: A GOOD LIFE

David Ewen

The Story of
Arturo Toscanini

NEW YORK: HENRY HOLT AND COMPANY

92625–0211

Printed in the United States of America.

"So striking a phenomenon as Toscanini is hardly explicable by known laws. He is one of those splendid anomalies whereby nature, from time to time, deigns to rehabilitate the human race."

—*Carl Engel*

Contents

Appendixes

Introduction: The Conductor's Art

As arts go, that of conducting is comparatively young. Up to about the middle of the nineteenth century, the conductor had been little more than a time-beater. It is only since then that he has evolved into a great musical interpreter.

While the art of conducting is comparatively new, time-beating is as old as music itself. In the orchestras of ancient Egypt one or two musicians were selected to beat time by clapping their hands. In ancient Greece, one musician in every orchestra wore a heavy leaden shoe to stamp out the time. As centuries passed, the methods of time-beating varied. As Johannes Bähr wrote in a book published in 1719: "One man conducts with the foot, another with the head, a third with the hand, some with both hands, some again take a roll of paper, and others a stick." In the Sistine

Chapel in the sixteenth century, time was beaten with a roll of paper. A century later, Jean Baptiste Lully conducted at the Paris Opéra by pounding a heavy walking stick on the ground. One century after Lully, conductors combined time-beating with the playing of an instrument, designating the time with rapid motions of the head as they officiated at a harpsichord or organ (or, less frequently, at a violin or flute).

Some time-beaters were temperamental. Once during rehearsals Handel threw a kettledrum at one of his musicians and Lully smashed a violin in a fit of rage. Some time-beaters were men of outstanding musicianship who tried to bring to their perfunctory task something more than merely the functions of a metronome. These fine musicians tried to help their men give shape and form to the music they played and imposed stylistic refinements on their performances. Such a time-beater was Johann Sebastian Bach when he directed his singers at the St. Thomasschule in Leipzig in concerts of his masterworks. Such a time-beater, too, was Bach's contemporary, Johann Wenzel Stamitz. Stamitz' skill in integrating his musicians into a unified organism made his orchestra in Mannheim one of the musical phenomena of that period. "No orchestra of the world has ever surpassed the Mannheim orchestra in execution," wrote the eighteenth-century historian, Charles Burney. "Its forte is thunder, its crescendo is cataract, its diminuendo is a crystal stream babbling along in the distance, its piano a breath of spring."

Through such spasmodic exhibitions of temperament and musicianship the time-beater was slowly outgrowing his up-to-now limited functions.

The present-day conductor was born when the baton came into vogue early in the nineteenth century. Before that, it had been used sparingly, if at all. In 1820, Louis Spohr, the famous violinist and composer, came to London to direct the Royal Philharmonic. At the first rehearsal, he astounded the musicians by declining the first-violin seat offered to him from where all previous conductors of the Royal Philharmonic had led the orchestra. Instead he placed himself directly in front of the entire body of musicians. They were further astounded to see him take a little stick out of his breast pocket.

Spohr has told the rest of the story in his *Autobiography*: "Quite alarmed at such a novel proceeding, some of the directors protested against it, but when I besought them to grant me at least one trial they were pacified. The symphonies and overtures that were to be rehearsed were well known to me. . . . I, therefore, could not only give the tempi in a very decisive manner, but indicated to the wind instruments and horns all the entries, which ensured to them a confidence such as hitherto they had not known. . . . Incited thereby to more than attention, and conducted with certainty by the *visible* manner of giving the time, they played with a spirit and correctness such as, until then, they had never before been heard to play. Surprised and inspired by the result, the orchestra immediately after the first part of the symphony expressed loud its united assent to the new mode of conducting, and thereby overruled all further opposition on the part of the directors. . . . The triumph of the baton as a time-giver was decisive."

With the triumph of the baton, new importance was accorded the time-beater. He was no longer expected to play an instrument while indicating tempi. He could devote himself completely to guiding his players not only in time but also in style. Conductors now arose who brought to conducting the same exacting standards of interpretation that the great violinist or pianist did. There was Felix Mendelssohn, the famous composer, who directed the Leipzig Gewandhaus Orchestra from 1835 to 1843. There was Franz Liszt, equally famous as pianist and composer, who conducted operas and symphonies in Weimar from 1848 to 1859. There was Hector Berlioz who led concerts in Paris and later in London. Separately, and in different cities, these great musicians helped bring about artistic importance to conducting. By devoting increased effort at rehearsal time to phrasing, dynamics, nuances, and integration, these conductors helped to establish conducting as one of the arts.

The modern conductor made his bow in the person of Hans von Bülow. In 1880, von Bülow was appointed musical director in Meiningen. For the next five years he assumed sovereign command over his orchestra, and while doing so helped to make of conducting a complex and subtle art. "I am now making a thorough study of *Der Freischütz* so that I may know it by heart," he once wrote. "Only when one has thus mastered an opera . . . in which each nuance, each instrument, has its special determination and importance is it possible—so at least I think—to rehearse and conduct it." On another occasion he coined a now-famous aphorism: "A score should be in a conductor's head, not the conductor's head in the score."

The conductor had ceased being a time-beater. He was

now a fine and sensitive artist performing on the most complex, subtle, and demanding musical instrument in the world: the symphony orchestra.

Gustav Mahler once said that "there are no great orchestras, only great conductors." This aphorism, if not taken too literally, is a wise one. Arturo Toscanini conducting a high-school orchestra cannot produce great music, any more than Jascha Heifetz can by playing a ten-dollar violin. A *major* symphony orchestra, however, can be either a wonderful ensemble or a mediocre one, depending on the conductor who is directing it.

An orchestra is, after all, an organization of eighty or more men each playing his own music and usually oblivious of what is being played by the other men. He may be a very fine musician who can be depended upon to read the notes in front of him skillfully. But even this number of the finest performers in the world cannot make a great orchestra unless there is someone to blend them together into an artistic unity. The conductor must play on each section of the orchestra—the strings, the brass, the wood wind, the percussion—as a Horowitz plays on his Steinway, drawing from it the color, tone, nuances that the music calls for. Then the conductor must sensitively balance each section with the others.

It is not difficult to dissect the conductor's art and uncover the qualities that make for greatness. A conductor must have a sensitive ear that can pierce the most elaborate orchestral sonorities. He must know the score he is directing down to the smallest detail. Having both ear and brain, he must be able "to hear with his eyes, and see with his ears"; in other words, he must always be able to visualize the printed score when hearing his orchestra play, and re-create the orchestral sound when looking at the printed score. But ear and brain, however sensitive and developed, can never produce great music without another organ: the heart. After all, the emotional impact of the music must be felt by the conductor if he is to transfer it, in turn, to his men.

There are other qualities that a great conductor must have. He must have musical scholarship, for only by know-ing the musicological and historical backgrounds of the music he conducts can he fully understand its style. A great conductor changes his personality with each different kind of music he performs: he is sensitive and delicate in Haydn and brusquely vigorous in Richard Strauss, religious in Bach and sensual in Wagner, sophisticated in Debussy and in-nocent in Schubert. It is the mediocre or poor conductor who twists and distorts different musical styles to conform to his own temperament and personality. Together with musical scholarship must go a cultural background. Bruno Walter once remarked that "to know Beethoven you must also know *Hamlet* and Goethe." In other words, to inter-pret great music a conductor must have had his personality enriched through contact with great literature, art, or thought. To a narrow mind the notes in a piece of music are translated into pleasing sounds—and no more. To a great one, they become rich and throbbing with intellectual and emotional experiences.

Artistically, a conductor must have within him perpetual youth. The excitement and enthusiasm he first felt in coming into contact with a masterwork must remain with him each time he returns to it. A great conductor may play Beethoven's Fifth Symphony or Tchaikovsky's *Pathétique* hundreds of times in his career; but each time he plays it, the fires must burn hot within him and must kindle his performance. Only too often, unfortunately, conductors continue performing musical works of which they have long since grown tired, and the inevitable result is lackadaisical and stagnant performances.

Finally, a great conductor must have that magnetism of personality with which every leader is born. He must be able to arouse, excite, and inspire those who come into contact with him. His very presence must release electrical currents which charge the atmosphere around him and galvanize not only the men who play under him but the audience behind him.

A conductor's work is done at rehearsals. At concerts his gestures serve to telegraph to the men the tempo, nuances, balance, etc., which had already been carefully rehearsed. Each conductor must develop the baton technique which serves him best. Some prefer the most economical movements of body and hands; they carve the rhythm simply with the baton while suggesting subtle nuances through simple gestures of the left hand. Toscanini is one of these. Others go in for extravagant dramatics through body contortions and elaborate swaying of hands. The means are unimportant provided they do not distract and confuse the men; what is important are the results achieved by the means.

At the rehearsal, the conductor works out his interpretation. Interpretation does not mean putting into music retards or accelerations or dynamics not called for by the music, but imposed by the interpreter to heighten the emotional effect. Unfortunately, too many conductors are guilty of such indiscretions. Interpretation consists in giving expression to the inner voices of the music, in making the work flow freely and spontaneously, in endowing the melody with freshness and continuity of line and, finally, in performing a work with the understanding of its whole design, evolving each effect so that it does not obtrude from the general plan of the whole. The greatest performance is that which brings to life precisely what the composer put down on paper, no less and no more.

Over a period of many years, and in many different parts of the world, I have had the opportunity of hearing virtually every great conductor of our time, including men no longer alive—Karl Muck, Felix Weingartner, and Richard Strauss. I have also heard Toscanini hundreds of times—in concert, opera, and rehearsals; in New York, Milan, Bayreuth, Salzburg, Lucerne. There has never been a doubt in my mind that Toscanini is the greatest conductor of them all—an artist of such unique grandeur and of such monumental attainments that no one can be deservedly compared to him. This is not to imply that I have not been stirred, sometimes profoundly, by other conductors; nor do I wish to leave the false impression that Toscanini has never given an inferior performance. But no one has so consistently and so often given the quality of a revelation to his interpretations—be they of Mozart or Wagner, Beethoven

or Verdi, Schubert or Brahms. No one so completely penetrated the heart of the music he is conducting, evoking for
us its deepest and inmost secrets, so long hidden from us
by less inspired conductors.

To hear Toscanini direct music that is a thrice-told tale—
say *La Traviata* or *Aïda* or Schubert's *Unfinished Symphony*
—is to be made particularly aware of his incomparable
powers at interpretation. Suddenly, magically, the music,
grown tired and hackneyed through misuse by a generation
of mediocre conductors, is revivified, glowing and throbbing with a vitality we had forgotten or never knew it
possessed.

Under Toscanini's slashing baton, the music always
moves with a brisk, healthy pace; never is there anything
static about it. The orchestration always appears trans-
parent; often for the first time we are made conscious of
all the subtle, little strands of sound woven into the har-
monic and contrapuntal pattern. The melody is always
evoked from the musical texture with fullness and warmth
—never allowed to be smothered by the harmonies or
overwhelmed by the rhythms; there is the Italian sun in
that lyricism, the music literally *sings*. And yet, in dramatic
pages, the rhythm is inexorable, the chords descend like
hammer blows, and climactic surges are built up with overwhelming sonorous effect.

To these qualities—mobility, clarity, precision, poetic
lyricism—Toscanini adds a freshness of approach and an
enthusiasm that refuse to age. After all these years of conducting, he still plays a page of Beethoven or Verdi or
Wagner with wonder and awe at the genius that produced

it. It is not in him ever to accept such greatness complacently, and he does not allow his musicians to do so.

He brings one other trait to his music: the nobility and majesty of his conceptions, spacious as a cathedral, and often as spiritual. Hearing his performances we know that they could originate only with a great musician who is also a very great man.

1. "Il Genio—The Genius"

*L*IKE so many other Italian cities, Parma of the middle nineteenth century retained many reminders of the past. The remnants of the once encircling bastions, the Benedictine monastery with frescos by Correggio, the wooden Teatro Farnese, the Palazzo Municipale, and the Cathedral were some of the many heritages bequeathed by the fifteenth and sixteenth centuries. That historic past was being preserved not only in ramparts and buildings, but also in flesh and blood—the flesh and blood of Parma's wealthiest families. Their ancestries reached back to several generations of nobility, fame, power.

But the great and historic families of Parma had never included the name of Toscanini.

And they did not now include the household of which Claudio Toscanini was head.

1

Claudio Toscanini lived in that humble part of the city reserved for those who earned their living by their hands. He was a tailor. He was also a poor man; it was difficult making enough money and his family was often hungry. And he was an obscure man; the name of Toscanini was not known beyond Claudio's own neighborhood. But he accepted his lot stoically. "The Toscaninis," he would sometimes say with good humor, "have never been famous for either their wealth or their greatness." He accepted this fact as he accepted the weather. It was something completely out of his province to change or control.

He was a proud man who, despite his poverty, lived with dignity. The Toscanini children were always dressed neatly and cleanly—Claudio saw to that. But in hard times—and they were not infrequent—they had to get along as best they could with very little; Claudio would never think of asking anybody for help. The story goes that when the Toscaninis visited more fortunate relatives, the children were warned never to accept food: Claudio did not want anybody to suspect that they were in need of it.

His humble life did not allow many pleasures. But there was one pleasure Claudio could enjoy—good music, specifically the good music of grand opera. Extra coins were not plentiful in the Toscanini household, but somehow, in some way, he managed from time to time to find the price for a gallery seat at the local opera house. Bellini, Rossini, and Donizetti were his favorites. Their wonderful melodies touched his drab life with enchantment and their spell persisted long after the performance was over. Those evenings at the opera were the highlights of Claudio's life. He looked forward to them excitedly and would reminisce about them afterwards for weeks. In the company of a few friends he would make a long night of it. Long before curtain time, he would arrive at the theater with friends and a basket of food. During intermissions, he would eat his bread and cheese and drink his strong, red wine, and at the same time would excitedly discuss the good and the bad of the opera and the performance of the preceding act. When the opera was over, they would retire to one or another's home and talk some more about the opera and the singers.

Even when he did not have the price for an opera ticket Claudio was not deprived of music. He made it himself, in his own unschooled fashion. A few of his music-loving friends, most of whom could not read a note of music, would gather in his kitchen to sing the arias and choruses from their favorite operas, most of which they knew as well as their own names.

Thus, despite his comparatively low station, Claudio Toscanini managed to live with a certain measure of contentment and self-respect. And he expected his wife, Paola, and his children to do likewise.

Claudio and Paola Toscanini had three children, all girls, when a son was born to them at last on March 25, 1867. Most men have flights of fancy regarding the future of an only son, dreaming of a life for him of which they had been deprived, but not Claudio Toscanini. He did not fool himself regarding the fate that would await *his* Arturo. Arturo was not likely to become either famous, wealthy, or powerful, since in nineteenth-century Parma a man did not usually rise above the station into which he was born. The

intoxication of having a son did not distort Claudio's reason. In all probability, he felt, Arturo would have to earn
his living at a trade, like his father before him had done.
But Claudio would see to it that his son would grow to be
honorable, to live usefully if simply, to walk through life
with head high, to appreciate those finer things which even
a poor man could enjoy. Claudio would encourage, even
insist, that Arturo get the best education Parma could provide within Claudio's limited means. Claudio had a healthy
respect for learning (possibly because he had had so little
of it) and valued highly the place of culture in a man's life.

Since music was his own greatest interest, Claudio
brought his son into contact with it as early as possible.
He could not teach Arturo to read music or play an instrument, since he himself was musically illiterate; and he could
not afford to pay the fee of a music teacher. But he could
see to it that Arturo absorb the sounds of music. Whenever Claudio and his friends sang their beloved opera melodies in the Toscanini kitchen, Arturo would be brought
there. Placed near the stove, where he could be caressed
by the warmth, he would sometimes sit for hours, listening
silently to the singing.

Arturo was a docile child who sat without signs of re-
bellion—even if the music did not interest him at all. But
Claudio soon noticed that Arturo stayed in the kitchen
during the singing not because he had been placed there
by his father but because he wanted very much to stay.
As soon as the child could talk, he began asking his father
when these impromptu performances would take place. If
the occasion was near at hand, the child's delight was as
great as though he had been promised a coveted toy. On

the evening of the performance, the boy did not have to be brought into the kitchen. He was at his place near the stove, long before the first neighbor arrived. And when the singers came to a tender lyric passage—or a big, rousing chorus—his eyes immediately became radiant.

In his eighth year, Arturo was entered in the local grade school to begin his academic education. Stiff with cleanliness he would walk to school each morning—his books, and his lunch box, with bread and cheese, under his arm; like all Parma school children, he remained in school the entire day, returning home in the evening for the final meal.

At school, as at home, he was a quiet and tractable boy. He did what he was told to do, and usually did it capably. A few others in his class might learn their lessons more brilliantly than he did; some might be more adventurous in their search for knowledge. But Arturo's teachers appreciated his being a conscientious student, and they grew attached to him.

His teacher in the second grade, Signora Vernoni, was particularly drawn to him. She felt instinctively that there were depths to this serious, sensitive boy worth probing. She set herself the task of drawing the boy out of his reticent shell. She gave him poems to read. She told him stories of the great Italians of history and culture. To her satisfaction, she soon noticed that those poems and stories that the boy liked particularly he could commit to memory, word by word, after a single reading or hearing.

Once she had Arturo visit her at her home. There she led him to the piano and began showing him something about music. After that, it was musical instruction that the boy wanted most of all. He was always willing to forego the poems and the stories if, in return, he could spend the time at the piano learning how to draw from that formidable box beautiful sounds of music. He now came to Signora Vernoni's house at the slightest pretext. The moment he came, he slipped into the chair in front of the piano, painstakingly, and with the deepest concentration, trying to translate the casual few lessons he had been given into the opera arias and choruses he had heard at his home.

Signora Vernoni once said to him, after he had gone through an entire aria with an improvised accompaniment: "Say, aren't you already the little maestro!"

Signora Vernoni taught the boy what little she knew about music, and as the boy hungrily absorbed what she taught him and asked for more she realized that more professional instruction was now needed. She recognized something else, too. In making music, the boy was able to reveal his inmost feelings and moods. Music seemed to transform him from an introspective and self-centered boy into an uninhibited and happy one.

One evening, Signora Vernoni visited Claudio Toscanini. For some time now an idea had been germinating in her mind: to take Arturo out of grade school and enter him into the Conservatory. Her mission now was to sell that idea to Arturo's father.

"What makes you think that my Arturo is a genius?" Claudio asked simply:

Signora Vernoni's eyes flashed. "Who said anything about genius, Signor?"

"Then what are you trying to tell me?"

Signora Vernoni replied: "Only this—that your Arturo

is a musical child, no doubt about that. He seems to make music as naturally as we breathe. A child like that deserves the opportunity to study. What happens to him after he gets that opportunity—that, Signor Toscanini, is up to him and the Good Lord, and not up to us."

Claudio Toscanini was not at first receptive to the idea. He felt that before entering a Conservatory a boy should have, if not genius, well at least definite talent. Claudio was too modest a man to entertain the hope that talent could strike his simple household. Besides, Claudio knew that Arturo was not prepared to enter the Conservatory. Candidates for the Conservatory had to know a great deal about music before they could even be considered; his Arturo, he knew, simply did not have the necessary qualifications. And there was still another problem disturbing Claudio. Tuition was expensive at the Conservatory. How could an impoverished tailor—too poor to provide adequate food for his household—expect to meet the bills for all the years of a Conservatory education?

He offered his doubts, one by one, to Signora Vernoni; and one by one they were answered. She was a stubborn woman who could stand her ground and fight back.

Who were they to pass judgment on whether Arturo had talent or not, she argued hotly. Was not that a matter for properly equipped authorities—and only after Arturo had been given an opportunity to reveal his capabilities? And Signora Vernoni insisted that, while it was true that Arturo was not yet ready for the Conservatory, he could easily receive the necessary preparation in a short time. As for the tuition . . .

"Signor Toscanini, it may be that I have more faith in

your son than you have. But I have this to say to you. Give
Arturo his chance. After a while, he will win every scholarship the Conservatory has to give."

It may have been that Signora Vernoni's logic finally
won him over. Or it may have been that, in the remotest
recesses of his heart, Claudio permitted himself the luxury
of entertaining the hope that his son was all that his teacher
said he was. After all, he himself had had evidence of his
son's receptiveness to music. Signora Vernoni was merely
corroborating what he himself had seen. Claudio could not
suppress sudden flights of hope and fancy. It warmed
Claudio's heart to think of the possibility of his son becoming a musician—a musician trained at the Conservatory!—one who might even learn to compose wonderful
melodies out of the very air!

But Claudio could be stubborn, too, and would not allow
himself to confess immediately that he had been won over
to Signora Vernoni's way of thinking.

"I still think," he said softly, "that a good tailor is better
than a poor musician."

All the while, Claudio's wife, Paola, had been sitting in
a corner of the room sewing. She had said nothing, because
in the Toscanini household the big decisions were always
made by Claudio. But now she could remain silent no
longer. She said gently: "Signora, Arturo will get *his* opportunity. Nobody wants that more than Claudio himself."

So Signora Vernoni arranged for a local tuba player by
the name of Bonini to prepare Arturo for the Conservatory.
Arturo was taught harmony and theory as well as the basic
elements of piano playing. After the first few lessons there
remained little doubt that Arturo could make the grade.

Within a few months, Bonini pronounced Arturo ready to take his entrance examinations at the Parma Conservatory. Arturo passed them easily. He was nine years old, and his future course was already charted.

At the Parma Conservatory—where, a century earlier, Paganini, wizard of the violin, had studied as a boy—the students led a Spartan existence. The school day was so long and the after-school duties so plentiful that the boys had little time to themselves. Discipline was severe; all infractions of the rigid rules were severely punished. The boys were rarely allowed to emerge from the austere building where they lived, studied, ate, and slept, in virtual monastic seclusion from the world outside. The greatest privilege enjoyed by the students was a walk through the city, permitted twice a week. The food was frugal, hardly enough to satisfy the healthy appetites of growing boys. The usual meal consisted of bread and soup. Meat could be had only once a week but it was rationed.

Despite restrictions, deprivations, and severities at the Conservatory, life was by no means intolerable—especially to students like Arturo Toscanini to whom music was more important than food or freedom of movement. The students nicknamed him *"il genio—the genius."* The epithet infuriated the boy. His modesty was offended and he was painfully embarrassed at being the object of special attention. He fought savagely against its use. But the sobriquet clung to him. And it clung because it fit so snugly.

The boys regarded Arturo as a phenomenon. All of them were musical, otherwise they could not have been admitted to the Conservatory; some of them were outstandingly so.

But Arturo was in a class by himself. His appetite for music seemed insatiable. Nothing else seemed to hold any interest for him. He avoided the outdoor play and diversions the other boys of his age enjoyed. He never joined the twice-a-week excursions through the city, which meant a temporary escape from the school's restrictions. Those hours that Arturo did not spend in the classroom or in the study of his lessons, still belonged to music. He would haunt the Conservatory library to study the scores of symphonies and operas. He would lock himself in his room to write out transcriptions of opera arias, sonatas, choruses, or play them on the piano. He even sold his precious meat coupon to get money to buy scores. To have the masterpieces of the great composers in his room was more important to him than food.

Young people are seldom tolerant of excesses practiced by contemporaries. Ordinarily a child with Toscanini's singleness of purpose would have been subjected to ridicule and abuse. But there was something awesome, something even infectious, about Arturo's passionate intensity. It affected those who came into contact with him, and they were driven not to derision but to admiration and emulation.

Though the Conservatory strictly forbade indulgence in any musical activity other than that prescribed by the curriculum—and, although the Conservatory boys had usually preferred play and rest to extracurricular music-making—some of them were so infected by Arturo's enthusiasm for music that they, too, wanted to make music in collaboration with their friend. Secretly, they would collect in Arturo's room, their instruments furtively under their arms. There they would perform Toscanini transcriptions with Arturo conducting them. They would have to play softly—regardless of the dynamics demanded by the music—so that the authorities in a different part of the building might not hear them. It was not so much the music itself that was fun to them, or even playing. What was fun was to play it with Arturo. The boy seemed to set off sparks that ignited their interest and set it aflame. In some mysterious way they could not altogether understand, Arturo continually made of music an exciting experience. As he led them in the performance he seemed able to uncover new mysteries and subtleties and beauties in music in a way that the Conservatory professors, with their humdrum exercises, never could. Music ceased being rules found in textbooks. Under Arturo's driving enthusiasm, it became a vibrant, vital experience.

Even when these boys did not perform in their improvised orchestra, they liked visiting Arturo. They would sit around the piano and listen to him play the scores he had secretly removed from the library (just as secretly returned in a few days) or had bought with money obtained by selling his precious meat coupons.

Sometimes this secret music-making was detected by the Conservatory officials. All the culprits would be severely punished: they would have to live on bread and water for the rest of the week. And yet—the punishment notwithstanding!—the boys would soon be back in Arturo's room for more music.

Though Arturo was, from the very first, an exceptional student, it was two years before he earned a scholarship. This was partly due to the fact that the influential citizens

of the town invariably used their authority to get the awards
for boys of their own choice; and Arturo had no influence
working for him. But, at the price of terrible sacrifices,
Claudio Toscanini kept his son at the Conservatory, now
convinced by Arturo's progress and by the tales that came
to him from the school that he had made no mistake.

Arturo Toscanini's inexhaustible passion for and curiosity
in every facet of music could not fail to attract official attention eventually. Once this attention had been attracted, the
authorities could not fail to be impressed with the ease and
effortlessness with which the boy seemed to overcome any
musical problem put to him. After receiving the highest
marks in the solfeggio classes of Cerbella and Griffini,
Arturo's talent could not longer be ignored. For the next
seven years the school paid for his board and tuition.

It was in Carini's cello class that Arturo first revealed a
very special talent of his own—a phenomenal memory.
Time and again he would play his exercises without con-
sulting the music on the stand. On being questioned by his
teacher, he confessed that he was able to memorize a piece
of music after playing it through only once. Would Arturo
be willing to have his memory tested? The boy acquiesced.
First he was given a difficult piece of music to read at sight;
it was a florid virtuoso composition for cello which Carini
himself had written. After a single playing, the music was
removed from the stand; Arturo played it a second time
from memory. As a final and conclusive test, Carini showed
Toscanini the full orchestral score of Wagner's *Tannhäuser*,
an opera not yet very familiar in Italy. Toscanini read
through the overture, then, pushing the score aside, he sat

down to a nearby table and wrote out for Carini all the orchestral parts.

Carini watched the exhibition with incredulity. "The boys are right," he exclaimed. "You are *il genio!*"

Several years after Toscanini's graduation from the Conservatory, Carini was once again given evidence of his retentive memory. Carini visited Toscanini, who by now had achieved fame as a conductor, for a friendly chat. At one point in their conversation, Toscanini went over to the piano and played a composition.

"Do you like it?" Toscanini asked when he had finished.

"No, I don't," Carini answered emphatically. "To put it bluntly—it's terrible."

Toscanini's eyes flashed mischievously.

"To put it even more bluntly," Toscanini said, "you wrote it."

It was only then that Carini recalled that the music Toscanini had just played for him was the florid cello work that he had given Toscanini to read at sight at the Conservatory to test his memory!

Toscanini was graduated from the Parma Conservatory on July 14, 1885, nine years after he had entered. He received the highest possible ratings: 160 out of 160 in cello; 50 out of 50 in both piano and composition. His certificate read: "*con lode distinta*"—"with the highest distinction."

His teachers prophesied a brilliant future for him, though how brilliant that future would be not even they could possibly have guessed.

2. Debut

*F*RESH out of the Conservatory, Arturo Toscanini began thinking about his future. He knew he would have to make his living through music. He had been trained in nothing else. Furthermore, he was interested in nothing else. But in which field of music?

Though he had specialized in playing the cello at the Conservatory—and now played it well—he knew that a virtuoso career was not for him. To prepare himself as virtuoso a Conservatory student had to devote himself with complete dedication to the mastery of his technique. Toscanini's practicing had always been somewhat lackadaisical. Time and again he had preferred spending time poring over symphony scores rather than groping with double-stops, bowing, fingering. If he had won honors in the cello class it was only because his musical intelligence

14

inevitably unraveled problems, however difficult, and provided short cuts. Now that he was out of the Conservatory, his musical intelligence was still nimbler than his bow-arm and fingers.

Besides, even if he felt himself equipped to be a virtuoso, he would not have relished such a career. He liked to play the cello, but only to a degree. It never quite satisfied his voracious musical appetite completely. He preferred working with larger musical forces than a single instrument, and in works of larger scope than a piece for solo instrument. Only then was his musical imagination sufficiently stimulated. Not having such forces at his command, he preferred to study the scores of symphonies and operas and working out for himself the problems of interpretation they presented. And he continued making his own orchestral transcriptions of the music he loved.

Nor did he have any ambitions to be a composer. In Dacci's composition class at the Conservatory he had attracted some praise for a few charming—though by no means monumental—works for the voice, for the piano, or for orchestra. He himself conducted his own *Andante and Scherzo*, for orchestra, at a student's concert on May 25, 1884, and with considerable success. Today we may be inclined to wonder whether it was not the performance, rather than the music, that impressed the audience that day! Other little pieces—a *Lullaby*, for the piano, for example—were good enough to be issued by a Turin publisher. Despite these small successes (and Toscanini did not delude himself that they meant too much) he never seriously considered devoting himself to creative work. He sensed the inadequacy of the music he put down on paper, compared to that which he felt surging and swelling within him. As he studied the wonderful inspiration of a symphony like Beethoven's *Eroica* or an opera like Mozart's *Don Giovanni* he knew, with shattering impact, how futile it would be for him to try to walk in the footsteps of the gods.

Where then was he heading? He did not know. He could not even guess. But until he could know there was a living to be made. He had to support himself. Besides, things had been going badly at his father's home for some time now and he had to offer help.

In the last years at the Conservatory, Toscanini had been able to earn a modest income by playing the cello in local orchestras. First he was engaged by the Parma Royal Theatre, later by the Parma Municipal Orchestra. Playing the cello in an orchestra would, at least, answer the immediate problem of earning a living. He set out to look for a job.

It did not take him long to find one. He had already achieved a good reputation in Parma as an orchestral musician.

Claudio Rossi, a South American impresario, was then in Italy to form an opera company to tour his theaters in São Paulo and Rio de Janeiro. Toscanini had been recommended to him. Rossi signed Toscanini both as an orchestral cellist and as assistant chorus master.

The position appealed to Toscanini for reasons other than that it paid well. It would give him an opportunity to see something of the world outside of Parma, outside of Italy. More important still, it would give him the opportunity of traveling through another world—that of grand opera which he loved so passionately. Up to now he could explore *that* world only through the printed score, or through a gallery seat in the opera house. Now, he could grow intimate with it, as only a collaborator in the actual performances could.

Most of the members of Rossi's opera troupe were Italians, and they included some of the finest opera artists of the day. The principal conductor, Leopoldo Miguez, was not an Italian, however, but a Brazilian from Rio de Janeiro. From the very beginning, the conductor and his fellow artists were at odds. For one thing, the artists were not impressed with Miguez' musicianship, and often disagreed with him on many points of interpretation. For another, Miguez was frequently rude and highhanded in his relations with his artists. The realization that he was not receiving the respect owing to his position as conductor only intensified his arrogance and contempt. The two-month stay of the opera company in São Paulo widened the breach between conductor and the company until only open and undisguised hostility prevailed.

Miguez was planning revenge against the members of his company. But he was biding his time until they left São Paulo for his own native city of Rio de Janeiro where he was assured that public opinion would be on his side. The company opened in Rio de Janeiro with Gounod's *Faust,* a performance that went poorly. The following morning, Miguez published an open letter in the newspapers attacking all the musicians and singers of his company with blistering vehemence. He pointed out that it was due to their disloyalty to him, and their refusal to follow his instructions, that *Faust* had been performed so badly. And he concluded with the statement that since he was unable to get the co-operation he needed for better performances, he would conduct the troupe no longer.

Miguez' letter created an uproar in Rio de Janeiro, as Miguez knew it would. The music lovers of the city rallied to his defense. Miguez was after all one of them—a South American—while his adversaries in the company were foreigners. Besides, presenting as it did only one version of the situation, Miguez' letter showed the conductor to be a helpless victim of intrigues and jealousies.

The musical atmosphere of Rio de Janeiro became charged with electricity. It was obvious that very little would now be required to set off a veritable explosion.

For its second performance in Rio de Janeiro, the company had scheduled Verdi's *Aïda*, on the evening of June 26, 1886. Since Miguez had refused to conduct, his assistant, Carlo Superti, was called upon to substitute. A few minutes before curtain time, it became evident to the increasingly worried performers that the evening would not pass without incident. There was tension in the air. The audience was restive and noisy. In the gallery, small crowds had congregated in different sections to engage in whispered conferences. The lowering of the lights did not bring the customary hush of expectancy. On the contrary, the excitement seemed to be intensified.

When Superti walked from the wings to the conductor's platform, pandemonium was suddenly let loose in the theater. The audience rose to its feet and shouted defiantly at him. There were whistles and catcalls and the stamping of feet. In vain did Rossi, the impresario, try to quell the uproar. No sooner did he appear on the stage to address a few words to the audience when he was shouted off. In an attempt to placate the audience, Superti left the conductor's stand and gave over his baton to the chorus master, Aristide Venturi. But the audience was in no mood for appeasement. Venturi, too, was overwhelmed by the violence of the audience's verbal attacks and had to seek refuge.

There was commotion backstage, too. Some of the women singers were in tears, and one of them was even hysterical. One or two of the hotheads among the company threatened to go out into the theater and smash some heads, and would probably have done so if they had not been physically restrained.

Rossi paced the floor with anxiety not knowing what to do. To call off the performance that night would mean one thing: The company would no longer be able to perform in Rio de Janeiro. This would involve him in a staggering financial loss, and, to make matters even worse, would leave his artists stranded without funds thousands of miles from their home. And yet—how was it possible to give the performance amidst such a holocaust?

"Maybe another conductor will quiet them," ventured one of the singers without actually believing what she was saying.

Another remarked: "Maybe they're so tired of making noise out there that they will want to listen to some music, at last?"

A third added: "Unless someone goes out there and tries to conduct the opera, we are lost."

Rossi did not disguise his despair. "It's no use, no use at all. Out there they want to avenge Miguez and they are doing a thorough job of it. Besides, even if I wanted to, I couldn't send out another conductor. I just haven't another conductor."

It was then that one of the singers came up with a suggestion. It was a farfetched one, to be sure, and not likely to be feasible. But an emergency allowed for even farfetched suggestions. It was simply this: One of the cellists in the orchestra, Arturo Toscanini, had time and again proved to the company that he seemed to know all the famous operas by heart. When he helped rehearse the singers in his office as assistant chorus master, he never consulted the music. Besides, in working out certain passages he had revealed an unusual gift for musical interpretation. Why not make a last, desperate effort at placating the audience by sending out young Toscanini to conduct?

It was a fantastic idea, but Rossi was desperate and there was no alternative. He *had* to make every effort to give a performance that evening to save both his artists and himself.

"Very well," he said, "ask Toscanini to conduct."

Arturo Toscanini knew nothing of the pandemonium that was taking place that evening in the opera house, both in front and behind the stage. While the house was in an uproar, he was not in his seat in the cello section of the orchestra. He was not even in the opera house. Late that same afternoon, he had met a dark-haired, attractive girl. In the presence of her intense eyes and beguiling smile he forgot time and place. The hours passed. Suddenly he remembered that there was a performance that evening— and that he was late. Regretfully he parted company with his delightful companion. He rushed to the opera house, hoping that he might be able to slip furtively into his seat without being detected by either Rossi or Superti, protected by the darkness in the theater.

Making his way into the orchestra pit, he was suddenly confronted not only by the impresario, Superti, and Venturi, but also by some of the leading singers and the first-desk men of the orchestra. They were all shouting at him at the same time. With a sinking feeling, Toscanini felt that he was being taken to task for coming so late. His mind groped for some serviceable excuse.

But slowly and dimly he became aware that his fellow musicians were not attacking him at all. They were besieging him to ask a favor. Incredulous at what he was hearing, he soon realized what they wanted of him. They asked *him* to conduct that night! Their fate, they said, rested in *his* hands!

Conduct? The idea was outlandish. He had never in his life conducted an orchestra, except for his student efforts at the Conservatory. He knew virtually nothing of baton technique. Besides, how could he possibly lead singers and musicians without a single rehearsal?

But the great emergency was clarified to him. At last he knew that he had no alternative but take a chance. He did not doubt that he knew *Aïda* thoroughly; he had long ago memorized every single note of that opera. But he doubted if he had the necessary ability to keep the opera forces together. And he doubted if the audience, already so incensed, would be willing to accept a novice.

With his head bent low, and his baton under his armpit, Toscanini walked briskly through the orchestra to the con-

ductor's platform. As he made his way, the uproar in the
theater started anew. But this time it failed to gain momen-
tum. The sight of the thin, wiry youngster seemed to arouse
the curiosity and interest of the audience. Toscanini was
nineteen years old, but he looked much younger than that;
and an oversized frock coat, borrowed from a fellow musician, further accentuated his youth. A mere boy conducting an opera performance? The novelty of such a spectacle
dissipated the accumulated resentment of the audience.
The angry voices melted away. An intense silence suddenly
permeated the theater. Several thousand eyes were fixed on
the youngster who dared to fill the shoes of a maestro.

The baton descended with a crisp stroke. Later some of
the audience remarked that the young conductor did not
bother to open the score in front of him! The overture
began. The music rose and soared. The baton, in the hands
of the young man, was like a relentless weapon, now driving
the musicians, now cajoling them, now urging them on,
now restraining them, now inducing them to delicate state-
ments, now drawing from them powerful utterances. The
curtain rose on the first scene. And still the young man did
not open his score! The baton continued to drive and slash
as it gathered the forces of the orchestra and the singers.
The young conductor knew his music; that was evident
from the opening bar of the opera. There was not the slightest indecision in his demands and movements. The cues
were precise, the instructions explicit. He also had authority.
He seemed to know exactly what he wanted from the musicians at every moment, and he knew how best to telegraph
these wishes with succinct gestures of the left hand and
economical patterns of the baton. But there was something

else in that performance besides familiarity and authority. Electric currents seemed to be discharged from the personality of the conductor, to galvanize both musicians and audience. The atmosphere in the theater was magnetic. This was *living* music, alive in every bar, cogent and irresistible. The musicians, spurred on by the indefatigable drive of that baton, gave of themselves entirely.

That one so young should have been able to conduct a complete opera without making a fool of himself was enough to win the enthusiasm of that audience. That he should have been able to do this with the unfaltering command and self-assurance of a veteran made the feat even more astonishing. But that he should have been able to do this entirely from memory gave the performance a significance all its own. The audience's antagonism toward the opera company vanished long before the first act had ended. When the opera was finished, thunderous approval descended cataclysmically on the young conductor. Even the musicians in the pit and the singers on the stage joined in the electric excitement.

Exhausted emotionally and physically, his clothes wet with perspiration, his face flushed with excitement, Toscanini met the ovation diffidently. He was incredulous that this ovation should be for him, incredulous and embarrassed. For a moment he stood rooted on the conductor's platform. Then, clutching his baton tightly, he escaped and hid below the orchestra pit.

The newspapers of Rio de Janeiro did not fail to record the miracle that had taken place that night in the opera house. "Marvelous" was the word used by the critic of *Paiz*.

That performance saved the opera company. Voluntarily, Rossi revised Toscanini's contract. From now on, Toscanini was to be the principal conductor of the opera company, with a considerable increase in salary.

During the remainder of the tour, Toscanini directed eighteen different operas: Verdi's *Il Trovatore* and *Rigoletto*, Ponchielli's *La Gioconda*, Donizetti's *La Favorita*, Gounod's *Faust*, Meyerbeer's *Les Huguenots*, and several others less famous. And all the eighteen operas were conducted from memory. From what mysterious sources did a novice so suddenly acquire such an imposing repertoire? What strange and inexplicable powers were his that he could, the moment he stepped on the platform, make singers and musicians perform with such enthusiasm and vitality? These and other questions were asked again and again in the newspapers of South America as Toscanini conducted one opera after another, each with equal authority. He was, they said, a born conductor, a conductor—in the words of a Rio de Janeiro critic—"of ability, coolness, enthusiasm, energy."

Thus Toscanini had begun his career as a conductor. Appropriately enough, the world's most acclaimed conductor had inaugurated that career in triumph.

3. Journey to Greatness

DESPITE his phenomenal success in South Amer
ica, Toscanini did not find a conductor's post
awaiting him when he returned to Italy. As a matter of
fact, Italian music circles knew nothing of what had happened to him across the ocean. Only one small newspaper
in Parma had reported Toscanini's performances and then
only briefly. He was much too modest to publicize himself
or to display his South American clippings where it could
do the most good. When he learned that his mother had
carefully saved the few items that had appeared in the
Parma papers, he grew furious, and demanded that she
destroy them. And he was much too diffident to seek out a
conductor's job, even though that was what he wanted most.

He decided to return to humbler duties. He played the
cello in orchestras, as he had done before leaving Italy.

He coached singers. While fulfilling these tasks, he waited
patiently. He had already been given a miraculous opportunity to show what he could do without having to seek it.
Similar opportunities would surely arrive!

And they were not slow in coming.

Some of the singers in the troupe he had conducted in
South America had not forgotten what he had accomplished. They spoke with awe about his talent. By word of
mouth, they spread the story of his fabulous debut, and
his equally fabulous activity after that. One of these singers
was the tenor Nicola Figner. Figner was scheduled to appear
in Turin in a performance of *Edmea*, an opera by Alfredo
Catalani. Figner knew that Catalani had been dissatisfied
with the way that the conductor, Faccio, had performed
Edmea when it had been originally presented in La Scala
in Milan. Figner had also heard that Catalani was searching
for another conductor to take charge of the Turin performance. The tenor knew that Toscanini was the man for the
job, and he decided to bring him to Catalani's attention.
He arranged a meeting between conductor and composer in
a small Milan hotel.

Toscanini came first. While waiting for Catalani, he sat
down at the piano and started playing the opera score which
he found there, and with which he was still completely
unfamiliar. Soon absorbed with the music, Toscanini did
not hear the composer enter the room, nor notice that
Catalani had quietly seated himself in a corner. Toscanini
continued playing; Catalani listened. At last, the first act
was over. Toscanini shut the score. It was only then that
he noticed the presence of Catalani in the room. When
the official introduction was over, the composer asked:

"How long have you studied this opera of mine?"

Toscanini looked away. He explained, softly and quickly, that he had had no opportunity as yet to study the score. He had just been reading it for the first time.

"Incredible," mumbled the composer. "Absolutely incredible. I would not have believed it if I had not heard it with my own ears."

After that exhibition of Toscanini, Catalani needed no further persuasion to engage the young man as the conductor for his opera. That performance took place in Turin on November 4, 1886—Toscanini's baton debut in Italy. The newspapers of Turin might approach the coming event —the conducting of a modern opera by a young and comparatively inexperienced musician—with a degree of laughter. A cartoon, for example, showed a little boy in knickers clambering laboriously on to the conductor's platform, a baton in his little hand. Some writers described him facetiously as the "beardless *bambino*." But there was no laughter the moment the lights grew dim in the theater. Toscanini conducted from memory again, and the musicians were amazed at his consummate grasp of the music and his keen interpretative instincts. The audience reacted warmly to the impact of a powerfully realized performance upon them. Catalani was beside himself with joy; after the performance he embraced and kissed the conductor.

Nor was there any further laughter in the newspapers of Turin when they reviewed this event. One critic remarked unequivocally that Toscanini's Italian debut as a conductor was a "splendid dawn on the horizon of music."

Toscanini's success with *Edmea* meant that he could now exchange his cello for a baton. He was only too happy to do so, for conducting challenged and stimulated him in a way that the cello had never done. But before he said good-by to his instrument—and forever—he made a last appearance, purely as a sentimental gesture.

Verdi's *Otello* was scheduled to receive its world première at La Scala in Milan on February 5, 1887. The master of Italian opera, Verdi, now in his seventy-fourth year, was present at both the final rehearsals and the first public performance. To Toscanini, who regarded Verdi with reverence and awe, the première of Verdi's latest opera was an occasion in which he felt he had to participate. He asked for a job as the second cellist in the La Scala orchestra and was accepted.

Since truth is often less dramatic than fiction, it cannot be said that Verdi, seated in the first row in the theater during the rehearsals of his new opera, was able to recognize in the cello playing of the young and wiry musician in the orchestra one who was soon destined to become his greatest interpreter. Verdi *did* notice Toscanini, but not with admiration. In one passage Toscanini played softly as was designated in the music. Verdi stopped the performance and asked the second cellist to play a bit louder. Toscanini felt that the request was unreasonable since it negated the written instructions; besides, Toscanini's own tastes and instincts had dictated that *piano*, and only *piano*, was required in that passage. However, Toscanini had no intention of arguing the point with the master, feeling as he did that the wish of the composer was the ultimate law which no musician should violate. He played louder, and Verdi was satisfied.

After the *Otello* première, Toscanini's day as an orchestral cellist was over. In 1887-1888 he served as the conductor of an opera troupe that toured the smaller Italian cities. To each town he came unknown and unheralded. In each town he transformed each of his performances into a decisive personal victory. Although his career was only beginning, the critics were already marshaling their superlatives to describe his conducting. "The orchestra accomplished miracles," wrote the critic in Casale, after Toscanini had led Meyerbeer's *L'Africaine* after only four rehearsals! "Under his magic baton the orchestra was marvelous," said another critic about his performance of Thomas' *Mignon*. At Dal Verme on November 19, 1888, he conducted a world première for the first time in his life: Antonio Cagnoni's *Francesca da Rimini*. A writer for the Milan *Gazetta Musicale* spoke of the "perfection of execution," adding, "I wish many composers might have such an interpreter."

The critics were only echoing what audiences everywhere felt about this new conductor. Whenever one of his performances came to an end, the public gave him a thunderous ovation. They said even then—what Toscanini audiences were to say again and again during the next half century: operas conducted by Toscanini sounded as they had never quite sounded before.

Assignments came thick and fast.

Once again, Toscanini toured the smaller Italian cities extensively. Besides these performances, he appeared as an assistant conductor to Mascheroni at the Liceo Theatre in Barcelona during the season of 1890-1891. His popularity in Barcelona grew so great that the envious Mascheroni contrived to get for Toscanini the less desirable operas of the repertory; and when these less desirable operas suddenly became popular because Toscanini conducted them, Mascheroni saw to it that Toscanini's activities were drastically curtailed.

During the winter of 1891, Toscanini was the principal conductor of the Carlo Felice Theatre in Genoa. In this position, he took in his stride both the established masterpieces of the operatic theater, and new and infrequently heard works. On February 18, 1891, he led one of Catalani's recent operas, *Loreley*. But whether Toscanini directed the familiar or the unfamiliar, he always revealed a fantastic knowledge of the score and an instinctive understanding of what the composer tried to put down on paper. After the performance of *Loreley*, Catalani wrote to Toscanini: "No one else can divine and interpret me as you do."

Though his performances inspired virtually extravagant praises from the critics, and evoked from audiences the most ardent responses, Toscanini's rapidly growing success was not achieved without battle.

His glowing performances might find him many admirers everywhere. But his personality—his savage idealism, his intransigeance, his refusal to compromise, his intolerance with mediocrity—made enemies. Even then, with his place in the music world still to be made, he stubbornly refused to work with incompetent singers or orchestral musicians, some of whom were enjoying a comfortable sinecure. Even then he would not pamper the stars, many of whom resented bitterly that a young man so new to his profession should dare to tell them that they were not singing correctly. Toscanini also turned a deaf ear to powerful publishers who would use their influence with him to further

a new artist or a new opera. Only the merits of the artist or
the opera could count with him; the fear of offending an
influential publisher could not alter the situation as far as
he was concerned. He was ruthless with impresarios who
economized by reducing the size of orchestra or chorus, or
by curtailing the number of rehearsals. When asked to
make such concessions, Toscanini stoutly insisted that he
would not conduct.

He was as implacable about little things as big ones.
Those who worked with him could not understand how
he could concern himself so seriously with minutiae, not
realizing that for him no detail of any performance was
too negligible to be ignored. Sometimes he felt that a singer
did not look the part and refused to allow him to appear in
the opera. He fought continually about the scenery, the
costuming, and the lighting. Even the way a theater was lit
was his affair. Once he insisted that no nonessential lights
be used in the theater while the performance was in progress. When his wishes were defied, he angrily smashed the
light on his own stand with his fist, rushed furiously backstage, and swore he would not return to conduct until his
order was carried out.

At one time, he was scheduled to give an orchestral concert with the orchestra of a small-town opera house. The
impresario, reluctant to remove the props from the stage
for this occasion, insisted that Toscanini conduct his concert from the pit. Toscanini, however, was not satisfied with
the acoustics, and insisted that, if there was to be a concert,
he would have to lead the orchestra on the stage. The impresario made a pretense of yielding. But when concert
time arrived, the props were still on the stage; and the

musicians were seated in the pit. Toscanini fled from the theater, went home, and locked his door. Not prayers or entreaties could prevail on him to return. After a delay of half an hour, the concert was postponed and the money refunded to the disappointed audience.

Many of those who came into direct conflict with him—conflicts from which he would emerge victorious, otherwise he would not perform—resented such an implacable will that could not bend to expediency. Influential musicians whom he offended began saying bitterly that his quick success had inflated his ego. Toscanini, they would remark with mockery, felt that he was a king who could do no wrong. These people preferred interpreting Toscanini's integrity and idealism as self-aggrandizement.

There were even times when Toscanini came to grips with his audiences, however much they might appreciate his wonderful performances. One issue was that of encores. Toscanini from the very first consistently refused to allow a singer to repeat an aria, however much the audience might shout for it. Encores, he insisted, shattered both the unity and the mobility of an opera. His refusal broke a tradition of long standing in the Italian opera house. It was a tradition dear not only to the hearts of singers who felt that these demands for encores were personal tributes but to audiences who also liked hearing their beloved arias repeated when they were sung well. In Palermo, Sicily, the audience insisted long and loudly for the repetition of one of the arias, shouting its demand at the young conductor. Toscanini, his hands on his hips, faced the audience with eyes flashing defiance, insisting by his silent gesture that he would not proceed with his performance until quiet was restored. For a moment it appeared as if some of the more inflammable in that audience were at the explosion point; a few hotheads rose in their seats and appeared ready to descend on the conductor with physical attacks. But Toscanini remained on his stand, looking at the aroused audience angrily but without fear. Obviously he had no intention of yielding ground in the fight. His courage so impressed the leader of the local Mafia, the band that ruled Sicily at the time, that he left his box, walked over to Toscanini, and put his arm around the young conductor's shoulders. This gesture was intended not only as encouragement to Toscanini but also as a deterrent to any possible attack from the audience. Quiet restored at last, the opera could continue—but, of course, *without* the encore.

On another occasion Toscanini was directing a performance of *Otello* in Pisa when a bomb was thrown on the stage from the gallery; the culprit was believed to be a singer who, discharged by Toscanini for incompetence, was seeking revenge. The bomb itself did little damage. But for a moment it appeared as if panic would erupt in the auditorium. Coolly and collectedly, Toscanini asked his orchestra to play the Royal March and the Garibaldi Hymn. The strains of this patriotic music helped to restore order.

This stubborn refusal by Toscanini to give encores in the opera house remained a live issue between conductor and audiences for many years. "We warn you," one opera lover wrote to him anonymously, "you had better execute encores without being begged to!" But Toscanini never gave in on this point. The example he has set and for which he has fought so bitterly has been largely responsible for the fact that in many of the world's opera houses, including our own Metropolitan Opera, encores are not permitted.

These provocative personal traits, so inextricably bound up with his artistic integrity, go a long way to explain the phenomenon of Toscanini's emergence to greatness as a conductor without a preliminary period of growth, evolution, and experience. This does not mean that in those days he brought to the masterpieces of music that maturity and wisdom that were to characterize later performances. His concept of Beethoven and Wagner and Verdi was, with passing years, to become enriched as he subjected their music to continual and unceasing reanalysis, and as he himself, through learning and through experience, became enriched as a human being. But even then, at the beginning of his career, he had qualities which made him unique among conductors: an amazing memory, that made it possible for him to learn a new score virtually overnight, and know it at once with the familiarity that usually comes only after a long association; an equally amazing ear, that could detect the slightest defection in a performance; a magnetism of personality that seemed to infect whoever came into contact with it; a passion for exactness and accuracy; an integrity that put art above any personal considerations. Even in those days, there existed for him only one standard: the highest. A demoniac force in him, that he could neither suppress or control, led him continually and restlessly to seek perfection at all costs.

While he was busily filling his engagements as a conductor, Toscanini was also coming into personal contact with Italy's leading operatic composers. And all of them were at one time to consider him their ideal interpreter.

His debut in Italy took place with Catalani's *Edmea*. From that time on a bond existed between conductor and composer that was to continue until the latter's death in 1893. In 1892, Toscanini conducted a second Catalani opera, *Loreley*, in Genoa, and received the composer's humble gratitude. When a performance of Catalani's most famous opera of all, *La Wally*, was scheduled in the composer's home town of Lucca in September of 1892, Catalani once again insisted that Toscanini conduct. This event was a major triumph for the composer; it was the last opera he was to witness. Toscanini's affection for Catalani and his respect for *La Wally* were later revealed when he named two of his children after characters in the Catalani opera— Wally and Walter.

Another prominent Italian composer with whom Toscanini was early thrown into contact was Alberto Franchetti, whose opera *Asrael* had already achieved international fame. (It was seen at the Metropolitan Opera House in 1890.) Franchetti had written a new opera, *Cristoforo Colombo*, to commemorate the 400th anniversary of Columbus' discovery of America. The first two performances of this opera were heard in Genoa, in October of 1892, with Mancinelli conducting. Mancinelli was compelled to go to Spain to fill an engagement; for a while it seemed that Franchetti's opera would have to be shelved, since no other conductor in Italy knew the score well enough to direct it. Toscanini, with his ability to learn new works quickly, provided the only alternative, and Franchetti begged the young conductor to help him. Toscanini locked himself in his apartment and, through the night, studied a score which he had neither seen nor heard before this. The next evening the scheduled third performance of *Cristoforo Colombo* took place under Toscanini. Without the benefit of a single rehearsal, he led from memory a work which he had not even known twenty-four hours earlier! The audience, which included Verdi, was amazed by this incredible achievement.

After that, Franchetti was one of the most ardent admirers of Toscanini. After a particularly beautiful performance of *Cristoforo Colombo* in Treviso, in October, 1893, Franchetti jumped on the stage and, in full view of the audience, embraced the conductor.

Both Catalani and Franchetti were famous when Toscanini first became associated with their music. But there were other opera composers in Italy who were as yet unknown when Toscanini began directing their music, but who were later to achieve international fame.

In January of 1890, Toscanini directed a performance of an opera called *Le Villi* in Brescia, an opera which had received its première performance six years earlier under another conductor. *Le Villi* was the first work of a composer then still comparatively obscure: Giacomo Puccini. In March, 1894, Toscanini conducted still another early Puccini opera, *Manon Lescaut* (with which, incidentally, Puccini had realized his first success). Puccini was present at that performance of *Manon Lescaut* and was greatly impressed by what he heard. Now a successful composer, Puccini was in a position to dictate where his next operas should be performed and by whom. It was Toscanini he selected to conduct the première of his latest opera, *La Bohème*. That historic performance took place in Turin on February 1, 1896 and was extraordinarily successful. "Toscanini," Puccini later said of him, "conducts a work not just as the written score directs, but as the composer had imagined it, though his hand failed him when the moment came to write what he heard so clearly in his head."

In 1892, a new opera by still another unknown composer was sent to Toscanini by the publisher Sonzogno. Toscanini was so impressed by the dramatic power and the lyric beauty of the work that he accepted the assignment of directing its première. That new opera was another milestone in contemporary opera, for it was *Pagliacci* by an unknown Neapolitan composer named Ruggiero Leoncavallo. *Pagliacci*, introduced by Toscanini at the Dal Verme Theatre in Milan on May 21, 1892, was a sensation. In the excitement of discovering a new opera, one rich with beauty and emotion, the Milanese did not forget that part of the success that evening belonged to the indefatigable conductor who had prepared and presented it with so much care and devotion.

It was in the same year that Toscanini had led *Pagliacci* that he conducted a Wagnerian opera for the first time in his career. Since that performance marked the appearance of one of the world's greatest Wagnerian conductors, its importance cannot be overestimated.

Toscanini had heard Wagner's music for the first time as a student at the Parma Conservatory when a performance of the *Tannhäuser* Overture took place in his city. And it will be recalled that it was by writing down the full orchestral score of this overture that Toscanini had proved to his teacher, Carini, the extent of his ability in memorizing music. The *Tannhäuser* music, so much more complex and so different in style from the Italian operas Toscanini knew and loved, puzzled him. He reacted coldly to it. Even after he had studied the cello part of the overture he still found the music complex and uninteresting.

But five years later Toscanini played in the orchestra when *Lohengrin* was introduced to Parma. Now a much more mature musician—behind him lay several years of study of German music—Toscanini suddenly discovered the greatness of Wagner. Here is the way he himself put it many years later: "I had then the first true, great, sublime revelation of Wagner's genius. At the first rehearsal, and from the very beginning, the prelude gave me magic, supernatural impressions, with its divine harmonies, which revealed to me an entire new world, a world that no one dreamed existed, before it was discovered by the supernatural mind of Wagner."

When *The Flying Dutchman* was performed in Italy for the first time—in Turin, in 1886—Toscanini helped coach the singers. And it was in this very same opera that Toscanini received his initiation as a Wagnerian conductor: in Turin in March of 1892.

Three years after this, Toscanini conducted a second Wagner opera, *Tannhäuser*, in Genoa. The local critic reported that this performance was a major Toscanini triumph. "The orchestra was marvelous in fusion, precision, color, chiaroscuro, full of power, élan, and spirituality." So successful was Toscanini in *Tannhäuser* that he had to repeat his performance eight times that season.

In the same year, 1895, Toscanini inaugurated the winter season of the Teatro Regio in Turin with the first performance in Italy of *Götterdämmerung*. The magnitude of this event in Italy's musical life can best be emphasized by the fact that a special orchestra was assembled for Toscanini for the occasion, a special booklet was printed and distributed in Turin to explain the music drama, and visitors came to Turin from all parts of Italy to hear the performance. There was even a newspaper correspondent representing America! The occasion was a triumph for Wagner, whose sublime music, unfolded to an Italian audience for the first time, had its inescapable effect. But it was also a triumph for the conductor. One critic went so far as to say that not even in Bayreuth—the shrine of the Wagnerian music drama, where it was to be expected that the last word in authoritative Wagnerian performances be spoken—could a better performance be heard. "Under the intelligent and skilled direction of Toscanini, there is such a fusion, such accuracy of interpretation and execution, such vital and youth spirit!" exclaimed the critic of *La Stampa*. "Toscanini has prepared and conducted the whole opera with great love and rare artistic understanding. He was able to obtain from his orchestra every finesse of color and expression and magnificent *pianissimi* and *crescendi*."

On February 1, 1897, Toscanini conducted his first *Tristan and Isolde*, and, one season after that, his first *Die Walküre*. (It was also in 1897 that Toscanini married Carla dei Martini, a ballerina who danced in some of the operas he conducted in Turin. Mrs. Toscanini immediately retired to devote herself completely to her husband and his career.)

When he became musical director of La Scala in Milan for the first time, he was to inaugurate his regime not with

an Italian opera, as might have been expected, but with
Die Meistersinger—evidence of how much Wagner had
come to mean to him. At La Scala he continually dedicated
himself to Wagnerian music drama with wondrous results.
Indeed, so celebrated and so wonderful were these performances at La Scala that even a German critic, Paul
Marsorp, was to concede Toscanini's pre-eminence as a
Wagnerian interpreter, at the same time remarking sadly
how shameful it was that a German had to travel to Milan
to hear Wagner performed properly.

But about La Scala—and about Toscanini's ultimate
victory as a Wagnerian conductor at Bayreuth itself, the
very fountainhead of Wagnerian music—much more will
be said later.

Meanwhile, Toscanini was achieving no less striking successes in a world apart from that of opera: symphonic music.

He had been conducting orchestral music at intermittent
periods, and in various cities, from the very beginning of
his baton career. And in orchestral music, as well as in
opera, his recognition as an aristocratic performer was to be
immediate.

On March 20, 1896, he gave a concert in Turin, the program of which included Schubert's Symphony in C major
(No. 9), and shorter works by Brahms, Tchaikovsky, and
Wagner. The ovation following this performance was so
thunderous that its echoes could, figuratively, be heard in
the city of Milan. There the directors of La Scala invited
Toscanini to give four orchestral concerts with their orchestra. At these concerts Toscanini played music by many
different composers of several different nationalities—

almost as if to prove his versatility. "He has surpassed the expectations of everyone," reported the critic of the *Gazetta Musicale*.

If there was still some doubt in some quarters that Toscanini was as distinguished in symphonic music as in operatic, that doubt was permanently dispelled two years later. In May of 1898, Toscanini was invited to direct a series of orchestral concerts at the International Exposition in Turin. He conducted for two months in the spring, and for another two and a half months in the fall. In all, he gave forty-three concerts in which 133 works by fifty-four different composers were heard. He gave first performances for Italy, and performances of non-Italian works rarely heard there; he shattered the insularity of Italian music audiences by playing more music by German composers than by Italian (ninety German against seventy Italian). The fact that—because of the extraordinary variety of his programs, and the wide gamut of styles and countries represented—he often had to study a score a few hours before he began rehearsing it, did not deter him from exploring the new and the unfamiliar; nor did this fact prevent him from giving the most painstaking and authoritative performances.

But as the impresario Depanis noted wryly at the time, these Toscanini concerts were destined to be for Turin a fortune and a misfortune at the same time. A fortune— because the audiences that came to hear them taxed the capacity of the auditorium and enriched the treasury of the Exposition. A misfortune—because, paradoxically, in building Toscanini up so high, Turin had made him too big for itself. Toscanini's amazing achievements at the Turin Exposition made him even more famous than he had been up to now. Attention was attracted to him from all parts of Italy. There was no musical organization in Italy that would not seek his services. Indeed, the greatest of them all—La Scala in Milan—wanted him now.

Addio, Torino! . . . . Bon giorno, Milano! . . . .

4.   La Scala

fOR more than a century now—since 1778 when it was built at the command of Empress Maria Theresa of Austria, then ruler of northern Italy as well— La Scala had been one of the great opera houses of Europe, and the greatest in all Italy. But it had come upon sad days. In July, 1897, in a sudden wave of economy, the city administration withdrew the annual funds which up to now had provided support to that great institution. The opera house had to suspend operations. The resentment of the Milanese, who loved their opera, was great. One irate music lover posted a huge sign on the closed door reading: "Closed on account of the death of artistic sensitivity, civic pride, and plain common sense." Notwithstanding this resentment, the opera house remained shut for more than a year.

In the summer of 1898, the city administration had a

change of heart. Financial support was restored to La Scala. The machinery was at once set into motion to reopen the theater.

To restore that grandeur which for so long a time had belonged to the opera house—a grandeur so ignominiously snuffed out for a year and a half—the directors decided to bring to La Scala the man now generally conceded to be Italy's greatest conductor. Would Toscanini be willing to take over the post of permanent conductor? Toscanini said he would, if the conditions at La Scala would allow for the kind of performances he wanted to give. To assure him that he would have his way, the directors appointed Toscanini not only permanent conductor but artistic director as well.

Toscanini proceeded to carry out the authority now vested in him. For the opening performance, to take place on December 26, 1898, Toscanini had selected Wagner's *Die Meistersinger*. The choice of this opera was in itself a forceful indication that Toscanini was determined to place artistic considerations above the box office. La Scala audiences would have much preferred a familiar Italian opera to a comparatively complex, long, and unfamiliar work from the foreign repertory. But Toscanini chose that opera which he felt would immediately set the standard he hoped to maintain at La Scala; and he ignored the likes and dislikes of his audience.

No sooner did Toscanini announce the choice of his opera when he let it be known that, despite its great length, he would not tolerate the cuts that previous Italian performances had allowed. The audiences had to hear the opera as Wagner intended it to be heard.

For a month the artists of La Scala were subjected to rigorous rehearsals the like of which they had never before experienced. The driving passion of the new conductor for perfection was a force that simply refused to be curbed by impediments. Day after day, hour after hour, Toscanini worked with the singers, the orchestra, the scenic designers. Even details—the singing of a single voice in the chorus, or the acting of a single extra—absorbed his attention. Now he was on the conductor's stand working over a phrase until the musicians were limp with fatigue, now on the stage, demonstrating how one of the singers should gesture, now with one of the tenors at the piano.

He gave of himself unsparingly, and expected everybody around him to do likewise. The singers and the musicians complained bitterly that they were being overworked. But Toscanini was deaf to complaints and drove them even harder. The artistic vision he had in mind had to be brought to glowing life without a single concession to human frailty.

The result was a performance of *Die Meistersinger* the like of which had not been heard in Italy before this. There were some who, having heard the opera in Paris and Vienna, felt that it was as fine and exciting a performance as could be heard anywhere in the world.

If the artists of La Scala expected any relaxation on the part of the conductor, once opening night was behind them, they were doomed to disappointment. To Toscanini every performance had opening night significance. To each opera Toscanini dedicated himself anew, whether it was a towering masterpiece or a work of lesser significance. To each opera, Toscanini brought the same zeal, thoroughness, the same determination to realize the inmost dreams of its creator. When he reached short of that goal, he would not allow the opera to be performed. At one time he would not permit a performance of Bellini's *Norma* despite the many weeks spent in rehearsal (it had even reached the dress-rehearsal stage!) and a fortune had been expended.

"Thank you, thank you, thank you," was the message sent to Toscanini by Verdi after a particularly eloquent performance of *Falstaff*. Verdi was speaking for himself. But he might have served as the spokesman for every composer whose operas were being revitalized at La Scala through Toscanini's performances.

Toscanini remained at La Scala for three seasons. Despite the wish of his audiences for familiar Italian operas, he kept on giving them those works which he felt belonged in the repertory of a great opera house. There was Wagner, of course—more Wagner than any Italian opera house had given up to this time. Toscanini opened the 1899-1900 season with the Italian première of *Siegfried*, and that of 1900-1901 with *Die Walküre*. But there were other non-Italian operas besides Wagner. He introduced his audiences to such less familiar German works as Weber's *Euryanthe*, Humperdinck's *Hansel and Gretel*, and Karl Goldmark's *Queen of Sheba*. He also presented such Russian and French novelties as Tchaikovsky's *Eugen Onegin* and Berlioz' *Damnation of Faust*. He gave first performances of new Italian operas: *Anton* by Galeotti, *Zaza* by Leoncavallo, *Le Maschere* by Mascagni, *Germania* by Franchetti, *Oceana* by Smareglia. He did, of course, also perform operas dear to the hearts of La Scala habitués—the most popular works of Rossini, Verdi, and Puccini. But he would not permit the repertoire of his opera house to grow repetitious or static.

Through these three years he was the autocrat of the opera house. His will was imperious. What he wanted to accomplish was one thing and one thing alone. He wanted to give an opera as precisely and as faithfully as the composer wanted it given. That others could be less faithful to the artistic concept of the work was something he could not understand, and something he would never permit. A work of art was to him a thing holy, to be approached with humility and reverence. Less than complete dedication to its execution was to him sacrilege.

Once one of La Scala's famous sopranos held a note longer than the score specified. Angrily and impatiently, Toscanini broke in with the orchestral interlude. In a fit of anger, the soprano exclaimed: "Maestro, it is I who am the star of this performance." Toscanini answered simply: "Madame, stars are found only in heaven."

The famous tenor, Tamagno, insisted on singing a passage in Verdi's *Otello* in a tempo other than that desired by Toscanini.

"But maestro," Tamagno insisted, "Verdi himself taught me how this was to be sung—and at the première!"

Toscanini thundered: "There is only one tempo—the correct one!" Then Toscanini reminded Tamagno that he, too, had been present at the première of *Otello*—having played in the orchestra—and that he clearly remembered the tempo Verdi wished to be used.

Since neither the tenor nor the conductor would yield to the other, Verdi himself had to be called in to adjudicate the issue. Verdi settled it once and for all by telling Toscanini: "You are, of course, right, maestro. Your memory is fantastic."

Toscanini remained true to the composer's intentions by following to the letter everything that was in the score—dotting every "i" and crossing every "t," so to speak. But sometimes this was not enough. Sometimes, in bringing out the very essence of a composer's thought, Toscanini had to go beyond the printed instructions. Once, while directing the Italian première of Verdi's *Pezzi Sacri*, Toscanini inserted a slight diminuendo in one of the passages of the *Te Deum*. Verdi came to him and asked: "But how did you know, maestro, that a diminuendo was called for?" Verdi went on to explain: "I have always wanted it that way, but did not dare to put it into the music for fear that other conductors would allow the music to drag."

On another occasion, Toscanini was rehearsing a new opera, Smareglia's *Oceana*. During the rehearsal, the composer entered the theater and listened. The scene over, Smareglia told Toscanini that the tempo that had been adopted had been too rapid. Always ready to carry out the wishes of a composer, Toscanini had the scene rehearsed again, this time in a slower tempo. When the second rehearsal ended, Smareglia told Toscanini: "No, no! It is you who were right. The music sounds much better in your tempo than in mine—and yours will be the correct one from now on."

On January 27, 1901, Giuseppe Verdi died in Milan at the patriarchal age of eighty-seven. Italians everywhere mourned the death of their greatest composer. But few mourned him so deeply or so personally as Toscanini. He might venerate the music of other composers more—say that of Beethoven or Wagner—but to the music of no other composer did he bring a more all-embracing love and a more personal attachment.

Toscanini had been musically nurtured by Verdi's music all his life. He had heard the arias and choruses of the early Verdi operas in the kitchen of his father's house, sung by his father and the neighbors. He had studied the early Verdi scores in the library of the Parma Conservatory. He had made his debut as conductor in a Verdi opera. He had conducted all the great Verdi operas—even the early ones like *Il Trovatore* which had temporarily fallen into disrepute in Italy but which he helped to restore to popularity through his luminous performances. He had played the cello in the première of Verdi's *Otello*. And many critics believed that Toscanini's performances of Verdi's last opera, *Falstaff*, were his very best.

He grew to know the man through personal contacts, just as he had grown to know the composer through his music. He was even to hear the master honor him with singing words of praise again and again. The bond that tied him to the great man of Italian opera grew tighter all the time.

Many incidents emphasize Toscanini's reverence toward Verdi. There was the time Toscanini was asked to participate in a festival of Verdi operas. He said it would be a privilege for him to do so; but he could do so only on the condition that he were not paid for his services. To be paid for an act of homage to Verdi seemed a sacrilege to Toscanini. This episode, incidentally, has an amusing epilogue. A rival Italian conductor, long jealous of Toscanini's popularity, was also invited to conduct at that festival. He insisted that he was to be paid more than Toscanini, even if it were only one lira more. To his consternation, after he had given his performance, the conductor received the payment of—one lira!

And now the great Verdi was dead. With the homage of a disciple, Toscanini set about to honor Verdi's memory. Four days after his death, Toscanini conducted a Verdi program in which two of Italy's greatest tenors participated —Tamagno and Caruso. He played selections from earlier operas through *La Forza del destino*—almost as if Toscanini now wanted to remind his compatriots what they had forgotten, namely, that there was greatness and inspiration even in Verdi's earlier works.

Three weeks after this concert, the body of Verdi was conducted to its final resting place; almost a quarter of a million people lined the streets to pay a last silent tribute to the composer. This cortege was accompanied by a chorus from Verdi's *Nabucco*, conducted by Toscanini. That same night, Toscanini led a performance of *Elisir d'Amore* at La Scala. The opera completed, Toscanini once again conducted the chorus of *Nabucco*—his final farewell.

Toscanini's regime at La Scala came to an end—temporarily at least—with dramatic suddenness.

Even as many of the singers and the musicians of the company did, the La Scala audiences found much to complain about in their irascible, despotic conductor. They did not for a moment doubt the fact that his performances were among the best that the La Scala had given within the memory of the oldest operagoer. They did not deny that he was a shining asset to the opera house. But in spite of the fact that they admired his genius, they nursed grievances against him.

They could not understand, for example, his displeasure at the ovations they gave him. He fled from applause and cheers as if they were a plague, refusing to take more than one or two perfunctory bows. They were inclined to look upon the reticence as some kind of snobbery; they felt that Toscanini regarded them with highhanded condescension. Since they had never before been confronted with modesty of this kind in their conductors they could not understand that Toscanini had an almost psychopathic dread of deflecting to himself the credit that he felt was due only to the composer.

He was continually disregarding their comforts and desires! They did not like Toscanini's insistence on playing the new, the unfamiliar, the foreign. They did not like it when, following Wagner's explicit instructions, he refused to allow an intermission between the first and second scenes in the third act of *Lohengrin*. But what they objected to most of all was Toscanini's inflexible rule against encores: again and again they tried to get an aria repeated through obstreperous ovations, and again and again Toscanini had defied them.

On the closing night of the 1902-1903 season, the audience's antagonism got out of control. Zanatello was given a particularly effusive ovation after an aria in *The Masked Ball*. This time the ovation did not subside when Toscanini sternly raised his baton to continue the opera. It did not even subside when he turned around to fix his electrifying eyes on the audience. For a few minutes, Toscanini waited for the noise to die down. When it failed to do so, he ran out of the opera house, muttering oaths under his breath. Another conductor had to finish the opera. The next morning, Toscanini left Italy—setting sail for South America where he had to fill an engagement. But so intense was his fury that he announced he would conduct in La Scala no more.

Eventually the terrible anger was dissipated. The following June Toscanini conducted the Turin Orchestra on the stage of La Scala. The audience cheered him; he encored one of the orchestral numbers. A reconciliation between Toscanini and his Milanese public had apparently taken place that evening.

But not until the 1906-1907 season did Toscanini yield to the indefatigable pleas of the La Scala management to return to his old post. Toscanini returned—on his own terms, of course. The management posted signs that under no conditions would encores be allowed. And Toscanini's repertoire remained vital. A French opera—Bizet's *Carmen* —opened his season. There was a healthy quota of German operas, including the Italian première of Richard Strauss' *Salome*, Wagner's *Tristan and Isolde*, and Gluck's *Orfeo*. There was also a world première: Cilèa's *Gloria*.

This time Toscanini remained at La Scala only two seasons. Once again he helped shape La Scala history, through incandescent performances, and through the introduction of important novelties. His Italian première of Debussy's *Pelléas and Mélisande* (to which, incidentally, his audiences did not respond) has since been acknowledged to be one of the major artistic events in Italy of that period.

But the resentments, the quarrels, the clashes of temperament between conductor and personnel continued. And at last he felt that he could tolerate them no longer.

5. The Metropolitan Opera House

IN 1908, Giulio Gatti-Casazza, one of the directors of La Scala, was engaged by the Metropolitan Opera House of New York to share the manager's office with Andreas Dippel (Dippel to be in charge of the German repertory, Gatti-Casazza of the Italian). Gatti-Casazza urged Toscanini to come with him, to continue in New York the manager-conductor collaboration that had been artistically so fruitful in Milan.

New York had been trying to get him for some time now. Toscanini could have had, for the asking, either the direction of the Metropolitan Opera or of the New York Philharmonic Orchestra. He wanted neither post, since at the time he felt that the place for him to work on a permanent basis was in his own country. But by 1908 Toscanini had grown so weary of struggles within La Scala that the prospect of a change of scene grew increasingly appealing. Perhaps in New York he would, at last, be able to work as his conscience dictated, without obstructions, without interference, without envy and feuds, without misunderstandings! Gatti-Casazza had promised him that he would do all he could to obtain for Toscanini those working conditions that he found so necessary. Toscanini, finally, agreed to come.

When, immediately after his arrival in New York, Toscanini inspected the facilities of the Metropolitan Opera House with minute scrutiny, he expressed satisfaction with the materials with which he would have to work. Indeed, the Metropolitan—then in its twenty-fifth year—was one of the great opera houses of the world. Behind it lay an already rich tradition of opera-making. Between 1884 and 1889 it had given distinguished performances of German operas under the artistic direction of Dr. Leopold Damrosch. From 1897 to 1903, the "era of great casts" was established by the impresario, Maurice Grau. The great roles in opera, and even many of the lesser ones, were filled by stars of the first magnitude: the de Reszke brothers, Emma Eames, Lilli Lehmann, Sembrich, Nordica, Plançon, Schumann-Heink, Maurel. From 1902 to 1908, the regime of Henrich Conried witnessed the American debuts of Olive Fremstad, Geraldine Farrar, and (most important of all) Enrico Caruso, and the American premières of Richard Strauss' *Salome* and Richard Wagner's *Parsifal* (the latter performed for the first time anywhere outside of Bayreuth). In 1908, Heinrich Conried left, and Gatti-Casazza replaced him. And the Metropolitan stood at the threshold of a new era.

Gatti-Casazza's long and fruitful reign as the director of the Metropolitan Opera House began on the same evening that Toscanini was introduced to the American public: November 16, 1908. The opera was the same one with which Toscanini had made his conductorial debut—*Aïda*. But with what a difference! In the cast now were some of the greatest voices of the generation: Enrico Caruso, Louise Homer, Emmy Destinn. With Toscanini in the pit, coalescing the many brilliant parts into an integrated artistic whole that was greater than any of its parts, that performance of *Aïda* was, as one critic put it, "the finest of Verdi ever given in New York." Toscanini was referred to by Henry E. Krehbiel as an "artist, an interpreter, a recreator in the best sense." Richard Aldrich described him as "a strenuous force, a dominating power, a man of potent authority, a musician of infinite resource."

One month later, on December 10, Toscanini conducted his first Wagnerian music drama in America—*Die Götterdämmerung*. Once again the New York music critics were beside themselves. "To him went the cometlike glory of the night," wrote the critic of the New York *Sun*. "*He* was the nucleus; the *Götterdämmerung* was the tail."

Those Toscanini performances ushered in a new epoch for the Metropolitan Opera House, an epoch sometimes aptly referred to as "the golden age of opera." Golden, indeed! Across the stage of the Metropolitan there strode some of the greatest artists of the generation. Enrico Caruso at his very prime, bringing to the famous Italian opera role a touch of sheer magic. . . . The incomparable Tetrazzini, the queen of the *prime donne* . . . Emmy Destinn, goddess of the Wagnerian music drama . . . Olive Fremstad,

Johanna Gadski, Walter Slezak, Geraldine Farrar, Frieda Hempel, Antonio Scotti, Louise Homer. . . .

And greatness on the opera stage was matched by greatness on the conductor's stand. During his first year at the Metropolitan, Toscanini shared the limelight with Gustav Mahler, whose baton achievements with the Vienna Opera had already become legendary. He, too, was a musician cut from the same cloth that made a Toscanini: of the highest standards, flaming idealism, impeccable integrity, priestlike devotion to his art. He, too, was intransigeant and despotic in carrying out his artistic mission. Between them, Toscanini and Mahler carried the lion's share of the repertory, and carried it majestically.

But in the season that followed, Mahler was gone. Toscanini was the principal conductor. He was to remain that for the next six years. His work called for a Herculean expenditure of energy since he had to add to his own varied repertoire many of the operas identified with Mahler. But, his increased burden notwithstanding, he remained indefatigable in striving for ideal performances.

The pattern of his La Scala regime repeated itself in New York. There were glorious, sometimes incomparable, performances whenever Toscanini conducted. But in achieving these performances Toscanini once again had to fight savagely to break down resistance. Pampered prime donne and adulated tenors—many of them of world renown—could not take gracefully to his biting criticisms, especially since they were administered at rehearsals before the entire company. Their vanities were punctured and their egos deflated—and this they would not tolerate. Besides, Toscanini worked them in a state of fatigue. At one time one of the most famous stars came to Gatti-Casazza to complain about the way Toscanini was abusing him. "What can I do?" Gatti-Casazza asked sadly. "He abuses all of us. He abuses *me*."

And Toscanini *did* abuse Gatti-Casazza, his old friend and fellow worker, and in a few years they were not even on speaking terms. The most bitter conflict centered around the question of rehearsal time. Toscanini demanded more and more rehearsals, refusing to recognize the practical problems of an opera house which could devote only so many hours (and these to its entire repertory) to rehearsing. Toscanini wore down the resistance of the management. But in getting his rehearsals, Toscanini aroused the antagonism of his associate conductors whose own rehearsal schedules were as a result severely curtailed.

As in La Scala, Toscanini's repertoire was flexible and varied. He performed twenty-nine different operas. The Italian repertory included the favorite works of Bellini, Verdi, and Puccini besides operas like Catalani's *Wally* and Franchetti's *Germania* which had become his particular specialties. He took over most of the Wagnerian repertory, the first time that an Italian conductor presumed to do so at the Metropolitan. He brought operas that, though famous in Europe, were new to the Metropolitan: Gluck's *Armide*, Mussorgsky's *Boris Godunov*, Dukas' *Ariane et Barbe-Bleue*, Montemezzi's *L'Amore dei Tre Re*. He also performed two world premières.

Of the two world premières, one was of particular significance. It was that of Giacomo Puccini's latest opera, *The Girl of the Golden West*.

In 1907, Puccini had been invited by Conried to help rehearse *Madame Butterfly* for its American première. While in this country, Puccini was commissioned by the Metropolitan to write a new work for that organization. Puccini wanted to write an opera with an American background. He attended all the Broadway plays he could in search of a suitable subject. One of these, a great success at the time, attracted him particularly. It was *The Girl of the Golden West,* an adaptation of a Bret Harte story by David Belasco. Puccini liked the Western locale of the play. "I should think that something stunning could be made of the '49 period," he said at that time. "I know the West only through Bret Harte and I admire him very much." There was something else about the play that appealed to Puccini. Its adaptator, David Belasco, had also been responsible for *Madame Butterfly,* having adapted the story of John Luther Long into a play which, in turn, was the source of Puccini's libretto. The resumption of a collaboration that had produced one of his greatest triumphs was an intriguing prospect for Puccini.

It took Puccini three years to complete the assignment. The première of the new opera—which took place on December 10, 1910—was one of the most glittering affairs of the opera season in New York. A world première by the foremost living opera composer—and with the composer himself present for the occasion—was an event inevitably inspiring no end of publicity and attention. The fact that this opera was also on an American subject intensified public curiosity and interest. The Metropolitan Opera rose to the occasion by assembling one of its most brilliant casts, headed by Enrico Caruso, Emmy Destinn, and Antonio Scotti. Toscanini, who had no equal as a Puccini interpreter, conducted. The audience was one of the most glamorous ever to attend a Metropolitan première. The elite of the social world came; the newspapers reported that the display of jewels and gowns was exceptional even for so traditionally lavish a setting as the Metropolitan.

The critics acclaimed Puccini's new opera, though it has since been recognized as one of the composer's less important achievements. But they were particularly rapturous about the performance, with Caruso and Toscanini coming in for the lion's share of the praise. "The presentation of the opera was one of Mr. Toscanini's masterpieces," wrote Richard Aldrich in *The New York Times*, "so vitalized, so full of detail, so broad in outlines, so finished."

Toscanini left the Metropolitan Opera permanently just as precipitously as he had La Scala. There had been no incident to send him away as there had been in Milan. It was true that there had been a good deal of friction between conductor and members of the opera company; but none of it was recent, none more excessive than that which had always existed.

A combination of circumstances influenced him. He had been working so hard that a prolonged state of physical fatigue brought him to the brink of a nervous breakdown. He felt—at least for the time being—that he could carry the burdens of an opera company no longer. Besides, it was now the year of 1915. Italy was at war against imperial Germany. Toscanini felt that his place was in Italy, and his efforts now belonged with the war.

The season of 1914-1915 over, Toscanini suddenly canceled two orchestral concerts which had been scheduled, and left for Italy, announcing at the time that he would never return to the Metropolitan. A long cable sent to him later by Otto H. Kahn—expressing the gratitude of the Metropolitan for his great achievements—went (strange to report) unanswered. All entreaties and offers for his return fell on deaf ears.

Back in Italy, Toscanini enlisted his baton in the war effort. He conducted operas and symphonies, all the proceeds of which were donated to various war charities. He directed patriotic concerts—sometimes even community sings!—to heighten civilian morale. Sometimes he even penetrated the actual battle front to conduct band concerts for the soldiers. On one occasion he led a military band on Monte Santo during an actual battle. The enemy fire was blistering; Toscanini and his musicians were protected only by a protruding rock. The music went on, while the Italian troops stormed the Austrian position; and it did not end until the Italians were victorious! For this, Toscanini was decorated by the Italian government. Sometime later, when Fiume was occupied by the Italians, Toscanini rushed there to direct a special concert celebrating the historic occasion.

He could display valor of a different kind, too, his own particular kind of valor. At a special soldiers' benefit concert in Rome, given by the Augusteo Orchestra in November of 1916, he directed the funeral music from Wagner's *Götterdämmerung.* Some in the audience were disturbed to hear music by a German. They expressed this resentment with shouts as the music was being played. "Are you play-

ing this German music to celebrate our dead?" one man
shouted at Toscanini. Toscanini shouted back: "I am playing music that belongs to the world." Then he threw his
baton away in disgust, stalked off the stage, and would conduct the Augusteo Orchestra no more.

When he did return to lead the Augusteo Orchestra it
was almost three years later. The war was now over. Sig-
nificantly and pointedly, Toscanini marked his return to
the orchestra with music by Wagner.

6. *La Scala Again*

fOR most of three years, between 1917 and 1920,
the La Scala was once again closed. During the
period of the war and of postwar readjustment there had
been no money for opera in Milan.

But in 1920 a movement arose to reopen the great opera
house. A group of wealthy art patrons stood ready to pay
all the bills, but on one condition alone: Toscanini would
have to return as artistic director.

At this time, Toscanini was being besieged with offers
by the world's greatest opera houses, some of them ready
to pay a king's ransom for his services. But the La Scala,
for all the anguish it had cost him, had a special place in
his heart. He wanted to return; as an Italian he preferred
being permanently attached to an Italian opera house. Besides, he was ever acutely conscious of the great traditions

of La Scala—where so many of Italy's great operas first saw the light of day; to be part of that tradition, to help to carry it on, meant a great deal to him.

But the patrons of La Scala had to be ready to meet his exacting terms. Toscanini was not thinking of his salary. Indeed, the salary he finally received from La Scala was much less than he had been offered elsewhere. And when, at the end of his first new season, a grateful management offered him a special bonus not called for in the agreement, Toscanini generously turned it over—and anonymously— to the general opera fund. What Toscanini wanted was free rein to run the opera house as he felt it should: on the highest possible artistic level. He wanted all the money necessary to buy the best musical and technical material available in Europe and to allow for complete rehabilitation of scenery and costumes. He needed assurances that he would get all the rehearsals he asked for. He wanted a free hand in the matter of repertoire. He planned to have all the old and familiar operas completely restudied by every member of the company; operas grown hackneyed through time might then become fresh and vital again. He would make the La Scala repertory the most adventurous in Europe through the introduction of new and unfamiliar operas.

To give Toscanini the limitless powers he demanded— and the money to implement those powers—the patrons not only appointed him musical director but also chief advisor to the financial syndicate. Virtually inexhaustible financial and artistic control was now placed in his hands. And he set to work with a will.

It took him eighteen months to get the opera house ready for the first performance, for he took personal charge of every detail. The acoustics of the house were improved upon. A new elaborate apparatus for the changing of scenery was installed. All costumes and scenery were redone, almost as if La Scala were a new opera house about to enter its first season. Musicians and singers were fastidiously screened, and only the best were engaged. The finest available technical staff was gathered to advise Toscanini.

At last, the La Scala could announce that it would reopen on the evening of December 26, 1921, with Toscanini's beloved opera, Verdi's *Falstaff*, as the initial attraction. Expectation ran high. It was known throughout all Europe that Toscanini had had his way in all things pertaining to that performance. And the occasion was—as everyone knew it would be—an artistic triumph of the first magnitude. Toscanini's interpretation of *Falstaff* was no novelty in Milan, and long had been considered the definitive one. But what was novel on that evening in 1921 was the completeness of the performance, a completeness never before realized in quite this way. The varied elements of acting, singing, orchestral playing, stagecraft, costuming, and scenery had been integrated into an indivisible artistic ensemble that made many in that audience feel that they were seeing the real *Falstaff* for the first time.

This time, Toscanini remained at La Scala for eight years, up through 1929. What years those were! The opera-making heard in Milan could be duplicated nowhere else. From all parts of the globe, opera lovers now made regular pilgrimages to Italy just to hear the Toscanini performances. Having heard them they left saying that they truly were incomparable.

In his first season Toscanini gave fifty-six performances

of five different operas: Verdi's *Falstaff*, Mussorgsky's *Boris Godunov*, Boïto's *Mefistofele*, Catalani's *Wally*, and Wagner's *Die Meistersinger*. Other operas were directed by other conductors; but always Toscanini was at hand to see that the opera house gave the best performances of which it was capable. The high points of the second season were Mozart's *The Magic Flute* and Wagner's *Tristan and Isolde*, both restudied, restaged, recostumed—presented as if they were new operas being heard for the first time. In subsequent seasons, Toscanini did a similar service to Wagner's complete *Ring* cycle; Debussy's *Pelléas and Mélisande*; Verdi's *Il Trovatore*, *The Masked Ball*, and *Otello*; Beethoven's *Fidelio*; Weber's *Der Freischütz*; Mozart's *Don Giovanni*; and Gounod's *Faust*. This recreation of operas long familiar was perhaps the crowning achievement of Toscanini at La Scala. It made possible the discard of some old misconceptions and errors perpetrated by tradition; it enabled a fresh examination of musical values both by the singers and the conductor; it encouraged the introduction of new stage techniques and concepts to the existing repertory.

There were new operas, too. Premières by some of Italy's foremost composers added a chapter of appreciable significance to Italian operatic history. They included: Pizzetti's *Débora e Jaéle* and *Fra Gherardo*, Respighi's *Belfagor* and *The Sunken Bell*, Alfano's *Sacùntala*, Boïto's *Nerone*, Giordano's *La Cena delle beffe*, and Puccini's *Turandot*.

Of the new operas, two were destined to be performed posthumously, and both were directed by Toscanini himself.

Arrigo Boïto's *Nerone* was presented on May 11, 1924,

six years after the composer's death. The occasion of this première was magnified into a moving memorial to one of Italy's most trenchant musicians: the fine composer who had produced the celebrated *Mefistofele*; the equally gifted librettist who had provided Verdi with the books for his last two great operas, *Falstaff* and *Otello*; the penetrating musical essayist and theorist.

The other opera—Puccini's *Turandot*—was heard on April 25, 1926, in an incomplete version.

Giacomo Puccini had died in Brussels, Belgium, on November 29, 1924, after an operation for cancer of the throat which was, at first, believed to have been miraculously successful. He died, however, after a subsequent heart attack.

Toscanini's grief at the loss of one of his dearest friends—and a composer whom he admired so profoundly—was intense. And, as he had once done for Verdi, he now set about to pay musical homage to Puccini. On December 3, 1924, he conducted the funeral elegy from Puccini's early opera *Edgar* during the funeral services held in the Milan Cathedral. "The grave, elegiac mood and the delicate expression of Puccini's music found in Toscanini the perfect interpreter," reported the *Corriere della Sera*. "Under the influence of his great emotion, Toscanini gave to his performance the color and expressiveness worthy of the magnitude of his interpretative art, and of the sentiment which inspired him in this sad hour."

But an even greater and more moving tribute to Puccini than this was planned by Toscanini. In the last days of his life, the master was at work on the final scenes of his last opera, *Turandot*. Franco Alfano, the gifted Italian composer, had been chosen after Puccini's death to complete the last duet and the final scene according to sketches left by the composer. But Toscanini—in a reverent gesture to Puccini's genius—would present the première of *Turandot* (which Puccini himself had designated for La Scala) exactly as it had been written. Toscanini knew that, shortly before his death, Puccini had said: "If I do not succeed in finishing the opera, some one will come to the front of the stage and say, 'Puccini composed as far as this, then he died.'" And Toscanini was determined to carry out the wish of the composer.

On the opening night of *Turandot*, therefore, the opera came to a sudden and abrupt close. The body of Liu, followed by her mourners, was carried off the stage. The piccolo sounded a piercing E-flat. Then, suddenly, there was no more. The action of the play was still unresolved, the music incomplete.

Toscanini put down his baton and turned to the audience. The tears were streaming down his face. "Here— here—the maestro died," he said.

Then the curtain came down slowly, sadly. . . .

Toscanini resigned from La Scala in 1929, but not because he was dissatisfied with conditions there. In fact, they were as ideal as they possibly could be. It was only because he felt that no longer did he have the mental and physical strength to continue the pace of the preceding eight years. Conducting operas throughout a long season is ever a serious strain. But this burden is negligible compared to that carried by an artistic director who personally supervises every detail of performance, and then keeps in-

.lefatigable watch over the activities of the other conductors. Toscanini had never spared his time or energy. Now
that he was no longer a young man—he had reached his
62nd birthday—he felt that he did not have a reservoir of
vitality to draw from. He was now continually weary, irri-
table, depressed. His nerves were taut. He felt the time had
come for him to call it a day—in the opera house, at any
rate. The conducting of symphonic music, to which he
now wanted to devote himself, would be much less of a
trial.

Before leaving La Scala (and he knew that he was now
leaving it permanently), he decided to take his entire company and its paraphernalia on tour to Vienna and Berlin.
It would be for him a kind of a valedictory.

Vienna and Berlin had always regarded their own opera
houses as paragons. Yet to the audiences of these cities,
Toscanini's performances of the Italian operas came as a
revelation. Paul Stefan, the eminent Viennese musicologist,
heard Toscanini conduct *Aïda* in Berlin. His reaction to
that performance was similar to that of all the leading
critics:

"That stupendous work perhaps brought me the brightest
illumination, moved me most profoundly, and certainly
provided me with the fullest safeguard against being able
to tolerate thenceforward the usual tepid, arbitrary, indifferent, and therefore fundamentally bad operatic performances. Now it was made manifest what Verdi had meant,
and what, in contradistinction to the Nordic distortion of
Verdi's style, is the true essence of such a work, nay of
Italian opera in general."

7.   The New York Philharmonic

AFTER 1929, the year of his retirement from La Scala, Toscanini's career changed character. Up to now he had associated himself primarily with opera, and only incidentally with symphonic music. Henceforth, it was orchestral music rather than opera which would be his major occupation. And his orchestral activity was from now on to be centered for the most part in America.

Toscanini's history as a conductor of symphonic music in America actually began when he was still at the Metropolitan Opera House. On February 21, 1909, he directed a performance of Verdi's *Requiem*, and on April 13, 1913, he led a symphonic concert the program of which included Wagner's *A Faust Overture*, Richard Strauss' *Till Eulenspiegel's Merry Pranks*, and Beethoven's Ninth (Choral) Symphony. The inevitable question arose among American critics at that time whether this man, whose pre-eminence in opera was an established fact, could duplicate his successes in orchestral music: there were not many conductors who were equally gifted in both fields. The question was answered decisively. Toscanini revealed "in the fullest measure the qualities of the great symphonic conductor," as Richard Aldrich wrote in *The New York Times* after hearing Toscanini conduct Beethoven's Ninth Symphony. And Aldrich articulated what most New Yorkers felt at that time, namely that "this remarkable" and "profoundly impressive performance" prompted the wish "that a way might be found for Mr. Toscanini to conduct more symphonic concerts for the New York public."

It seemed that this wish was to be fulfilled, at least partially, when Toscanini announced he would conduct two orchestral concerts with the Metropolitan Opera orchestra following the 1914-1915 opera season. But this venture was frustrated when, weary and nerve-wracked, Toscanini decided to sever his connections with the Metropolitan and to return to Europe.

In the winter of 1920-1921 Toscanini was again heard in this country as an orchestral conductor. This time he toured the United States and Canada with the La Scala Orchestra, giving 124 concerts, the first of which took place at the Metropolitan Opera House in New York on December 28, 1920. Actually, the orchestra he conducted on this tour was not that of La Scala, since the La Scala Opera had not been functioning for three years, but an organization improvised for the purposes of this engagement. It was, at best, a second-rate ensemble. Its performances revealed the careful training to which Toscanini had sub-

jected it. But there were perceptible flaws in its texture
which no amount of rehearsing could eliminate, because
the basic materials in the first place were not of the best.
The reaction of most American music lovers to these concerts was one of genuine regret that Toscanini could not be
heard in this country with an orchestra worthy of his genius.

Then and there the seeds of a project were planted: to
bring the mighty maestro to the head of one of America's
great symphonic organizations. They were not to flower for
several years. Toscanini, completely absorbed with launch-
ing his new regime at La Scala, could not entertain the
idea of working elsewhere. But offers from this country
kept coming. And as Toscanini grew more and more fa-
tigued with his onerous operatic labors, he grew more and
more receptive to the idea of becoming an orchestral
conductor.

In 1925, he accepted an invitation to serve as a guest
conductor of the New York Philharmonic Orchestra. The
Philharmonic was America's oldest symphonic organization,
and one of its best. Its eighty-four-year career was prolific
with great musical performances. Many distinguished conductors had had a role in the shaping of that career: Theo-
dore Thomas, Anton Seidl, Felix Weingartner, Richard
Strauss, Eduard Colonne, Vassily Safonov, Gustav Mahler,
Willem Mengelberg, and Wilhelm Furtwängler. In bringing Toscanini to America, the Philharmonic was carrying
on its long established tradition of enlisting the services of
Europe's greatest conductors.

The Philharmonic, then, had had a long and glorious
history when Toscanini came to conduct it for the first
time, on the evening of January 14, 1926. But on that eve-

ning it was to enter upon even greater musical achievements. It was the first time that America had had an opportunity to hear Toscanini conduct an orchestra of such
importance. For that occasion Carnegie Hall (bedecked
with flags) was overcrowded with the great and near-great
of New York's social, musical, and political life. That audience gave Toscanini a majestic ovation as he came to the
stage; it rose spontaneously to its feet and stood in homage.
But when the performance was over, the tumult and the
shouting rocked the auditorium.

The Toscanini madness had begun in America.

One season later, Toscanini was appointed permanent
conductor of the New York Philharmonic, sharing the
major part of the season with Willem Mengelberg. One
season after that—when the Philharmonic merged with
Walter Damrosch's New York Symphony Society to produce an even greater symphonic organization than formerly
—Toscanini became musical director. After 1929, Toscanini
devoted himself as selflessly and as completely to the New
York Philharmonic as he had up to now done to La Scala.

In New York, Toscanini now became an almost legendary figure. Fabulous tales—most of them true—were told
of his temperament, personality, genius. Toscanini could
do no wrong as far as his audiences and critics were concerned. Regardless of what he conducted, tickets for his
concerts were at a premium. The story is told that the rich
people of New York, who had been habitually turning over
their Philharmonic subscriptions to their servants, now had
to bribe them to get back the tickets for the Toscanini
concerts. Within Carnegie Hall the enthusiasm was always
unbridled. Few musicians anywhere, at any time, were

subjected to such a demonstration of uninterrupted and unadulterated adulation.

This adulation was found not only among the audiences but also among the musicians who played under him and came under his spell.

Toscanini was a tyrant who made them work harder than any conductor in their experience. His temper, when things did not go well, was cataclysmic. He would kick his music stand in fury, smash his baton, trample on his watch, sometimes even take off his alpaca coat and tear it to shreds, and thereby create a tension that was often nerve-wracking. His tongue was vitriolic as he subjected the musicians to withering abuse that was often downright insulting. "Pigs," he would shriek at the top of his voice, "you are all pigs!" Frequently he would shout at them in Italian because that language is richer in invective than English or German. Once when he did this he suddenly realized that his victim did not understand a word of Italian. Desperately Toscanini searched for an English equivalent to his tirade. But all he could come up with was: "You bad, bad man!" But when his temper would be spent, he would apologize for his harsh words and actions. "You see," he once explained, "God tells me how the music should sound—and sometimes you come in the way."

It was taxing to work with him, taxing every single moment of the rehearsal. But the musicians knew if he was hard with them, he was even harder with himself; they could therefore accept his abuse tolerantly. Often when a rehearsal failed to achieve the ideal he had in mind, he would blame no one but himself. "*Stupido, stupido,*" he

would yell, banging his fists at his temples. "Toscanini—
stupido!" Or he would leave the platform and sit in a
distant corner of the stage and whine to himself. Once
while conducting a symphonic work by Vincent d'Indy
he confused his men with his beat in a rhythmically complex passage. The result was a few moments of musical
chaos. Toscanini was so upset that, when the work was
finished, he escaped from the stage as if it had suddenly
become a profane place. Locking himself in the artist's
room, he gave way to his anger and pain. Eventually he
returned to the stage to continue the concert. Before beginning he said softly to the orchestra: "Gentlemen, forgive
me, *please* forgive me!"

In spite of the many trials of working with Toscanini,
the men literally worshiped him. For they continually saw
the grandeur and greatness of the man as no audiences
possibly could. Again and again they would suddenly, magically, see the masterpieces with new vision as Toscanini
emphasized this note, refined that passage, built up a
climax, clarified the sonority. One musician who played
under him put it this way: "Many of us had never drained
the last full measure of beauty from the familiar scores
until the hand of Toscanini painstakingly distilled it out
of us." As he tried to unfold his conception, Toscanini
analyzed, dissected, interpreted the music for his men.
Failing to clarify his intentions, he would posture, act,
burlesque, mime. He would rock his hands in cradlelike
fashion and tell the men: "Like this the music should
sound, like a mother rocking her baby to sleep." Or he
would drop his handkerchief to the floor and ask his musicians to try to simulate in their playing the limpid motion

of the cloth as it fell. He might fall on his knees and clasp his hands in prayer: "Pianissimo, gentlemen—please, pianissimo!" What he heard within him he tried to convey to his men, and by every means at his disposal.

What others quoted as legend, was in reality fact to the musician at rehearsal time. He was continually given evidence of Toscanini's fabulous ear. During even the most complex, sonorous passages, it could easily single out a flutist who did not play his passage staccato, or an oboist who slurred a phrase. The orchestra was also made conscious of his equally fabulous memory. There was the time a bassoonist came to him before the rehearsal to say that his instrument was broken and he could not sound the note of E-flat. Toscanini thought for a few silent moments and said: "The note of E-flat does not appear in your music today." Or the time when one of his violinists asked his opinion of a certain obscure work, and Toscanini sat down to the piano and played detailed portions of it—even though he had not seen or heard the music in more than fifty years.

The men were in the presence of his ceaseless drive for perfection, and were inspired by his relentlessness in accepting anything less than perfection. They knew that when he raged and fumed and swore it was not because of prima donna temperament, but rather because anything less than perfection brought him actual pain. A wrong note, and his suffering would be as intense as if he had been stabbed. At one time, a badly played passage sent him running away from the auditorium out in the street through the thick of traffic. He was oblivious of where he was going or why. A few of the orchestra men had to run after him and bring him back to the stage by promising they would play that passage better the next time.

Stefan Zweig, the famous writer, once put into eloquent words that which every musician felt and appreciated about Toscanini's drive for perfection:

"It is easy to understand why none but his intimates are allowed to attend these rehearsals, at which he knows he will be overcome by his insatiable passion for perfection. More and more alarming grows the spectacle of the struggle, as Toscanini strives to wring from the instrumentalists the visioned masterpiece which was to be fashioned in the sphere of universal audible reality. His body quivers with excitement, his voice becomes hoarse, his brow is beaded with sweat; he looks exhausted and aged by these immeasurable hours of strenuous toil; but never will he stop an inch short of perfection of his dream. With unceasingly renewed energy, he pushes onward and onward until the orchestra has at length been subject to his will and can interpret the composer's music exactly as it has presented itself to the great conductor's mind. Only he who has been privileged to witness this struggle for perfection hour after hour, day after day, can estimate the cost of the superexcellence which the public has come to expect as a matter of course."

No less awesome than Toscanini's search for perfection was his humility. Always he served music with complete and selfless dedication, relegating himself to a position far subservient to that of the creator. When a concertmaster asked him during a rehearsal: "Do you want a crescendo here, maestro?", Toscanini answered vehemently, "It is Brahms who wants that crescendo, not Toscanini!" It was only another way of emphasizing that not he but the composer must be served. He contemptuously rejected an elaborate floral wreath that was once bestowed on him by the Philharmonic management. "Wreaths are for corpses or prime donne, and I am neither," he explained. He tried to take as few curtain calls as possible, avoided any kind of personal publicity, fastidiously side-stepped attention. He could never really understand why he was such an object of adulation. "It is the composer who is everything, not the performer," he would say.

When rehearsals went well, he praised the composer, the music, the orchestra—never himself. It was impossible for him to believe that he had any share at all in the net result.

He was once rehearsing Beethoven's Ninth Symphony, when I was secretly present in the auditorium. Toscanini had given the musicians such a new and penetrating insight into the music—had so completely imbued them with the ideal of brotherhood of man expressed in the last movement—that they outdid themselves in their performance, and played the music as they had never done before this. When the rehearsal ended, the musicians rose spontaneously to their feet and cheered him. Toscanini flushed with embarrassment. Wildly he waved his hands at them to arrest this ovation. At last there was a lull, and Toscanini could protest: "It isn't me, men. . . . It's Beethoven. Beethoven is everything—Toscanini, nothing."

Just as La Scala had become the first opera house in the world under the direction of Toscanini, now the New York Philharmonic became the leading orchestra of the world. He fashioned the Philharmonic into an instrument of incomparable virtuosity and resiliency that could understand the slightest suggestion of his head, face, or hands, and could respond with the utmost sensitivity to his every wish. For beauty of orchestral sound and richness of sonority, for consummate technical mastery, for flexibility and integration, the New York Philharmonic under Toscanini was unique.

The music capitals of the world were soon to be made conscious of this orchestra's greatness. In the spring of 1930, Toscanini and orchestra toured Europe, the first time the New York Philharmonic was heard abroad. The 114 musicians (together with 38 wives, 9 children, 2 dogs, and 250 trunks) set sail on the S.S. *De Grasse* on April 23. Twenty-three concerts were scheduled; and each one of them had been completely sold out before the *De Grasse* left New York.

The first European concert took place in Paris on May 3 before as distinguished an audience as ever heard a concert at the famed Opéra. The audience was brilliant. It contained diplomats, financiers, musicians, actors, and writers. They came, heard, and were conquered. France's leading composer, Maurice Ravel, was there, and in his honor Toscanini led the *Bolero*. After each work the audience cheered for more than ten minutes and at the end of the concert the applause was near pandemonium.

From Paris, conductor and orchestra went on to Zurich, Milan, Turin, Rome, Florence, Munich, Vienna, Budapest, Prague, Leipzig, Dresden, Berlin, Brussels, and finally London. The scene might change; the reaction remained the same. Everywhere wild enthusiasm was let loose. In Zurich the cheering continued even after orchestra and conductor had left the hall. In Italy it was conceded that not since Verdi had that country been so stirred by a musical event as these Toscanini concerts. In London, the King of England and George Bernard Shaw personally congratulated Toscanini. Everywhere it was agreed that the New York Philharmonic was the finest orchestra in the world, and that Toscanini was the finest conductor. The marriage of the two inevitably resulted in a kind of orchestral music-making which even an older and richer musical civilization so proud of its own historic musical accomplishments could not duplicate.

8. Bayreuth and Salzburg

*I*N 1930, Toscanini was invited to conduct at the Wagner festival in Bayreuth, in Bavarian Germany. And once again he was to shape musical history.

Bayreuth was the sacrosanct shrine of the Wagnerian music drama. It was there that Richard Wagner had built his festival theater to realize his theories on the way his music dramas should be performed. It was there that his wishes were carried out down to the smallest details, as he personally supervised the productions of his mighty music dramas. It was in Bayreuth that he lived the last years of his life—at Villa Wahnfried, in whose garden he now lay buried. And it was in Bayreuth that his widow, Cosima— and, after her death, their son, Siegfried—carried on the traditions of Wagnerian performance set and established by the composer.

To every Wagnerite, Bayreuth is something of a holy city. It can only be guessed what it meant to Toscanini, who had devoted himself so passionately to Wagner's music dramas all his life, to conduct at Bayreuth. No doubt it was the realization of one of his inmost and deepest dreams, but one which he never felt he would realize. Never before had a foreigner been asked to conduct at Bayreuth. Jealous of their authority, the Germans were convinced that an art so Germanic as the Wagnerian music drama could never be successfully projected by someone who was not a German.

But the Toscanini performances of Wagner's music both at the Metropolitan Opera and La Scala had placed him with the greatest Wagnerian interpreters of all time, and far above many of those who officiated at Bayreuth. Bayreuth could no longer ignore him. It is no secret that Toscanini would have been invited to Bayreuth long before 1930 were it not for Karl Muck, the principal conductor at Bayreuth, who insisted that an Italian had no place among Bayreuth conductors. Eventually, Siegfried Wagner overrode Muck's violent opposition. Disregarding Muck, Siegfried Wagner sent out a call to Toscanini. The maestro was assigned two Wagner works for the 1930 festival, *Tannhäuser* (which had not been heard in Bayreuth for twenty-five years), and *Tristan and Isolde.*

Toscanini came to Bayreuth with the reverence of a religious pilgrim arriving at Rome or Jerusalem. He came not for money or for personal glory, but to serve the art of the mighty Wagner with humility and dedication, and to serve it at its shrine.

This was not an easy assignment. Traditions of performance were deeply entrenched in Bayreuth. Those who were part and parcel of Bayreuth's history felt that the ultimate truth of the Wagnerian art rested in their hands, and could not be subject to question or debate. Toscanini, of course, had his own conception; and when that conception differed from that sanctioned by Bayreuth he would not change. The music itself was his source—not habits and idiosyn-crasies evolved by different conductors through the years at Bayreuth—and to the music he would remain inflexibly faithful.

There were storms at the rehearsals. Some of Toscanini's tempi differed markedly from those assumed by preceding Bayreuth conductors. Toscanini insisted on giving Italian mobility and softness to some of the lyrical pages. A few musicians grumbled angrily that Toscanini was making of *Tannhäuser*, for example, an Italian opera. Some of the leading singers rebelled at having their interpretations sub-jected to criticism and change. It was not easy to break down resistance. But Toscanini broke it down here as he had done elsewhere, sometimes through volcanic outbursts of temper, sometimes through threats of withdrawing from the festival.

Eventually, of course, he had his way. And eventu-ally—as after many grueling rehearsals, his concept of the operas became integrated and fully realized—the musicians and singers conceded that he had been right after all.

Toscanini opened the 1930 Bayreuth festival on July 22 with *Tannhäuser*. That performance was given under the most unfavorable auspices. The principal tenor, Sigismund Pilinsky, left his sick bed to appear. Lauritz Melchior stood in the wings throughout the opera, ready to take over if Pilinsky collapsed. Toscanini was beside himself with worry because his wife had just broken her leg and was in a hospital. Siegfried Wagner, the artistic director, was not even at the performance as he was suffering from pneumonia.

Yet the performance betrayed no effects from these misfortunes. It had passion and tenderness, nobility and incandescence. It was quite true that Toscanini had brought the Italian sun into the opera. What the German pundits now remembered was that, of all Wagnerian works, *Tannhäuser* was the most Italian in temperament and style!

And what they were soon to learn—when, one day later, Toscanini turned from *Tannhäuser* to *Tristan*—was that it was the style of the work he conducted, and not his own nationality, that governed his artistic approach. For Toscanini's *Tristan*—an evocation of incomparable beauty— was true to the Germanic traditions of Wagnerian performance.

This writer, who was present in Bayreuth in 1930, was continually made aware of the complete way in which Toscanini dominated the festival. His picture was in all the shop windows, his name on everybody's lips. An incident which I witnessed characterized for me the attitude of Bayreuth toward the conductor. A group of children were playing outside the post office when Toscanini passed. The children froze in their play. At last one of them exclaimed a single word, the tone of which reflected his awe: *"Toscanini!"*

It is not difficult to understand why Toscanini's stature loomed so prodigiously. Bayreuth had undeniably degenerated badly after World War I, which left all of Germany financially destitute. Without the funds to buy the best available musicians, technical help, and materials, Bayreuth had to be satisfied with poor casts, old-fashioned scenery and costumes, and second-rate conductors. (Occasionally a performance under the direction of Karl Muck succeeded in rising far above the prevailing lethargy and mediocrity; but this was the exception to the rule.) For some years before 1930, Bayreuth had ceased to be a Mecca for many music lovers; even some of the German critics hesitated to go there.

But the eight performances by Toscanini—five of *Tannhäuser*, three of *Tristan*—revived Bayreuth's artistic greatness. Toscanini had neither the best possible singers nor the finest stage equipment. But he did have the power of his interpretative genius to bring vitality and fire and freshness and excitement to the Festival Theatre.

Toscanini, then, restored to Bayreuth the artistic greatness it had once known. And its glamour, too. This was authoritatively pointed out by Siegfried Wagner's daughter, Friedelind, in her book, *Heritage of Fire*: "Both from an artistic and box-office standpoint it was the most successful of all festivals since the war, and the *Tannhäuser* which Toscanini conducted was considered the most brilliant production of Father's career." It was Toscanini who had drawn to Bayreuth the most brilliant audiences it had known in several decades. (That summer, Bayreuth had 10,000 visitors—one thousand from the United States— who paid $250,000 in admission to the theater.) Perhaps never before had there been concentrated within so small a geographical area so much political power, wealth, and talent.

When Siegfried Wagner died on August 4, 1930, Toscanini was regarded as the logical—perhaps inevitable—candidate for the post of artistic director. Siegfried Wagner's widow, Winifred, was not only favorable to the Toscanini appointment; she regarded it as essential for the continued well-being of Bayreuth. But the unconfirmed reports of the Toscanini appointment—publicized throughout the world—created consternation in German music circles. That the first time the direction of Bayreuth should pass out of the hands of a Wagner only to go to an Italian, was a crushing blow to German chauvinism. Most of the leading German conductors felt as if they had been personally insulted. Karl Muck, as a matter of fact, made it known that he would no longer be associated with Bayreuth.

Whether because of tact, or because he felt that he was too old and tired to assume so enormous a burden, Toscanini did not accept the artistic direction of Bayreuth. That office went to Wilhelm Furtwängler, one of Germany's greatest conductors. But Toscanini did consent to return to Bayreuth for the 1931 festival to conduct *Tannhäuser*, and the music drama so long associated with Karl Muck, *Parsifal*. As in 1930, the personality of Toscanini, and the grandeur of his performances, brought to the festival proceedings a luster it would otherwise not have had.

During the 1931 festival, a disagreeable incident almost brought Toscanini's association with Bayreuth to a premature end. There took place on August 4 a concert commemorating the first anniversary of Siegfried Wagner's death. All the principal singers and conductors of Bayreuth participated. Toscanini willingly accepted one number on the program, but made the express condition that nobody was to be admitted to his rehearsal. Arriving for his rehearsal, Toscanini found the theater virtually crowded. Furious, Toscanini broke his baton and rushed out of the theater. He did not conduct at that festival concert, and might even have refused to conduct his other Bayreuth performances if Winifred Wagner had not placated him.

There was no festival in Bayreuth in 1932; traditionally, Bayreuth took off a full year after each two years of festivals. But in the 1933 festival, it was planned to have Toscanini play once again a major role: Among the music dramas assigned to him was the one he loved above all others, *Die Meistersinger.*

But Toscanini did not come to Bayreuth in 1933. Destiny, in the form of cataclysmic world events, dictated otherwise.

Away from music, as in it, Toscanini has lived with integrity, courage, and bigness of spirit. Unlike so many other artists, he has always been acutely aware of the social and political forces around him. And he has never hesitated to swim against the tide when decency impelled him to do so.

For a brief period, in 1919, he was tempted to enter politics in Italy. The demoralization and distintegration taking place in his land as the aftermath of World War I, impelled him to run for office with the Chamber of Deputies on a minority ticket. He wanted to do what he could to help restore order and civilized living to the Italian people. He ran for a party that promised most to the people both in material benefits and political freedom. His running mate was a then ardent Socialist by the name of Benito Mussolini. Both candidates were defeated. They received only 5,000 votes! Toscanini's brief excursion into politics came to an end. But his interest in his fellow man, and his espousal of the cause of freedom, have never been relaxed.

As is now well known, Benito Mussolini reversed himself after 1919, turning from a man-of-the-people into a ruthless autocrat who brought about Fascist rule in Italy. For almost two decades, Mussolini and his party subjugated the Italian people, crushing their liberties, trampling on their inalienable rights. Mussolini set a pattern which was later to be imitated and developed by Adolf Hitler in Germany.

Most prominent Italians in every walk of life scrambled on the Fascist bandwagon. They joined the Fascist party, gave the Fascist salute, sang lustily the Fascist anthem, *Giovinezza*. Composers, writers, painters produced works that glorified the ideals of fascism. Others lent the prestige of their names and reputations to further the movement, to give it dignity in the eyes of the outside world. Some did this because they believed in Mussolini, or benefited by his dictatorship, or were inflamed by the sudden resurgence of Italian power and chauvinism. Others accepted a bad situation tolerantly, felt too weak to combat it, and tried to find their place in the new society. After all, opponents of fascism were being ruthlessly annihilated. To survive, one had to give at least lip service to the regime.

Toscanini, however, made his position known from the very first, and without equivocation. He was against totalitarianism in any form, against tyranny wherever he found it. He refused to join the Fascist party. He refused to allow his name to be used in any way to dignify the movement. He openly expressed his antagonism to Mussolini and fascism whenever he could. At one time, Mussolini summoned Toscanini to the Palazza Venezia where, for a full hour, he tried to win him over to fascism. He tried bribery: Toscanini could have any office or honor he might desire. Toscanini's face remained a stiff mask. He tried threats: Mussolini had it in his power to force Toscanini to allegiance. Toscanini remained unmoved. At last, Toscanini spoke his true feelings, and the interview ended with stormy words. Had Toscanini been less of a world-famous personality, had he been less idolized by the Italian people, he would undoubtedly have suffered the fate met by other patriots who would not bend a knee to fascism: murder, or imprisonment, or torture. As it was, he was allowed to make his music without interference. But it was no secret that all the high officials of the Fascist party regarded him with resentment. Mussolini, for example, never attended a Toscanini performance. Toscanini was regarded as a kind of sore on the body of Italian fascism, a sore which simply had to be tolerated only because an operation might prove fatal to the entire body.

But there were times when Toscanini and the Fascists came into conflict.

When Toscanini came to Turin in 1930 during his tour with the New York Philharmonic, his concert was attended by the Princess of Piedmont. It was an ironclad rule that whenever royalty was present, the Italian anthem had to be played. It was also a rule in Fascist Italy that *Giovinezza* had to be performed with the national anthem. Toscanini was quite willing to conduct his anthem—but *Giovinezza,* never! For a while it seemed that the concert would not be given, since an impasse had been reached. The matter was finally settled by having a band appear on the stage before the concert and playing both the national anthem and the *Giovinezza*. When the band departed, Toscanini came on the stage to conduct the Philharmonic in the scheduled program.

Toscanini's stout refusal to play the *Giovinezza* was soon to have serious consequences.

On May 14, 1931, Toscanini conducted an Italian orchestra in Bologna in a concert devoted entirely to the music of Giuseppe Martucci. Toscanini was officially asked to play the *Giovinezza* before the concert, a request which he ignored icily. After the concert, he was waylaid outside the concert hall by a band of Fascists who attacked him with sticks and fists. So severe was the attack that it was believed to have brought on the bursitis of the shoulder from which Toscanini suffered so acutely for the next few years.

After the liberation of Italy, during World War II, the perpetrator of this attack was revealed to have been one Mario Ghinelli, who was forthwith, though belatedly, arrested for this offense. When Toscanini was informed of this arrest by an interviewer for the Associated Press, he expressed no bitterness for the offender, but only for the King of Italy who, at that time—for political expediency— was being kept in power by the Allied forces. "I had already forgotten the name of the man who offended me so slightly," Toscanini told the interviewer. "But I cannot forget the name of the degenerate King of Italy who has betrayed my country, who was the accomplice and the supporter of the Fascists in all their crimes against civil liberties, and who is one of the major ones responsible for this bloody war and the ruin and the misery of the Italian people."

A few days after the Martucci concert and the attack on Toscanini, a resolution was passed by artists and musicians of Bologna condemning Toscanini for refusing to play the anthem, and describing his action as "absurd and unpatriotic."

After that incident Toscanini would conduct in Italy no more. For the next few years he kept returning each year to spend his vacation at his beautiful home on one of the Borromean Islands near Stresa. But even these visits were soon denied him. His position kept growing more and more untenable. At one time, when he had once again expressed his contempt for fascism, he was kept a prisoner at his home as an enemy of the state, and released only when he promised he would do nothing further to embarrass the regime. He promised, and then left Italy determined not to return until the country was freed from totalitarian rule. Only his intimates knew how much it cost him to separate himself perhaps permanently from the land of his birth, his people, his language, his home.

This was the first great sacrifice Toscanini made for the sake of his political integrity. And it was not the last.

In 1933, the wave of fascism swept northwards from Italy into Germany. Hitler and nazism came to power, releasing brutal forces which made those of Mussolini's Italy anemic by comparison. The man who had so long fought tyranny in his own land—and at the risk of his life—was not likely to remain indifferent to oppression, intolerance, and persecution sweeping across another country. Toscanini did not

hesitate to put his name on a petition dispatched to Hitler
by leading American musicians, on April 1, 1933, urging
him to put an end to racial and religious discrimination.
The Nazi authorities reacted to this request in a character-
istic way. All the musicians who signed that petition—
among them were Walter Damrosch, Serge Koussevitzky,
Artur Bodanzky, Fritz Reiner, Ossip Gabrilowitsch, and
Harold Bauer—were henceforth to be boycotted in all German concert auditoriums. Nazi storm troopers ransacked
the phonograph record shops of several German cities to
smash all the Toscanini recordings they could find.

It was therefore out of the question for Toscanini to
participate in the 1933 festival in Bayreuth. The Nazis
would have been willing to accept him—in spite of their
resentment at his having signed the petition! They were
willing to shut their eyes to this "indiscretion" for the sake
of the prestige and money that Toscanini's presence would
attract to Bayreuth. But Toscanini let it be known that he
would never conduct in Germany as long as the Nazis were
in power. Winifred Wagner flew expressly from Bayreuth
to Paris where Toscanini was conducting to convince him
to change his mind. Nazism, she explained, was only a
passing phase, and its excesses would surely disappear. Why
allow the dirty boots of politics to trample the holy ground
of great art? The truth of the matter was that Winifred
Wagner, born an English woman, was as ardent a Nazi as
the most rabid storm trooper. But Bayreuth needed Toscanini, needed him badly—and she was willing to swallow
her pride and momentarily sacrifice her political beliefs to
get Toscanini back.

But Toscanini was not convinced by Winifred Wagner.

He could only think of the great musicians who had been thrown out of Germany, and of the great musical works that had been desecrated, all in the name of nazism. He could only remember that the heel of oppression was grinding into the neck of the German people. In such an atmosphere of persecution and hate, he could never conduct—not even his beloved *Meistersinger*, and at Wagner's shrine.

He did not go to Bayreuth in 1933. Instead, he accepted an invitation to conduct at the Salzburg Festival. Picturesque, rococo Salzburg in Austria—birthplace of Wolfgang Amadeus Mozart—had for many years been the scene for wonderful summer music. Europe's leading musicians came there to participate in performances of opera, symphony, chamber, and choral music; and music lovers from all parts of the world congregated to hear great music—sometimes twice, sometimes even three times, a day.

With Toscanini in Salzburg, the festival acquired new dimensions, and new significance. In 1934, Toscanini conducted only orchestral concerts. Beginning with 1935 he presented operas, too: *Fidelio* and *Falstaff*, in 1935; after that, *The Magic Flute* and *Die Meistersinger*. It was his performances of opera and symphony, from 1935 to 1938, that made Salzburg the number one festival of the world.

It was not musical considerations alone that led Toscanini to conduct Beethoven's *Fidelio* in Salzburg. *Fidelio* is Beethoven's proud affirmation of freedom. To Beethoven, Leonore was a symbol of liberation who, in setting her husband Florestan free from his cruel and undeserved imprisonment, likewise liberates all other prisoners. With some of the noblest music he ever wrote, Beethoven here spoke for those who are victims of tyranny. "Hail, hail the day, Hail the glorious hour, so long awaited yet unhoped for"—so sing the prisoners as they emerge from their cells, groping into the light. "When Justice joined with Mercy appears before us at the door of our grave." This is a majestic democratic pronouncement, such as is found in few places in music.

In conducting *Fidelio*, Toscanini, too, was sounding a message of hope to those who were being persecuted, and a threat to those who would be persecutors. Salzburg, it must be remembered, is on the very border of Germany; and Italy was not far away. Visitors from both lands came to Salzburg for the music. To these two countries, with their arrogant dictators—and to the visitors from these countries—Toscanini was now bringing the music of Beethoven as the challenge of free men against tyrants. Perhaps for this very reason, his performance of *Fidelio*—in that summer of 1935—was touched with nobility, humanity, consecration, and exaltation.

In Salzburg, Toscanini was to fight in more ways than one against the mounting tyranny of nazism. At one time there was serious consideration given by the Salzburg authorities to banning the broadcasts of all Bruno Walter performances at the request of Nazi diplomats. Bruno Walter had been the greatest of living German conductors before he was forced by the Nazis to escape to other lands. Walter's poetic and beautiful performances at the Salzburg Festival in Austria had been banned from the German radio networks, but they did penetrate into Germany itself and this infuriated the Nazis. The Nazis used all the political and diplomatic pressure they could to end the broadcasts.

They might have been successful but for Toscanini's intervention. He announced firmly that if Walter's broadcasts were banned, he would not remain in Salzburg. That threat brought the Nazi machinations to a sudden end.

Further, Toscanini frustrated the Nazi's maneuvers to relay broadcasts of *his* performances throughout the Reich.

On another occasion, Wilhelm Furtwängler—then an official representative of the Nazi government—gave several performances in Salzburg, including one of Beethoven's Ninth Symphony. Though Toscanini was often thrown into contact with Furtwängler, he ignored him completely, refusing to have anything whatsoever to do with a Nazi. In an effort to win Toscanini over, Furtwängler praised him for his recent performance of *Die Meistersinger*. Toscanini looked at Furtwängler contemptuously. Then, according to Otto Zarek in his *Splendor and Shame*, he said: "I wish I could return your compliment. But I have always thought that a man who gives his assent to a system that persecutes every independent-minded man and woman cannot interpret Beethoven's symphonies. For you Nazis have banned all manifestations of spirit, leaving nothing but forced rhythms and an excessive display of strength. And that is precisely what you did the other day with Beethoven's Ninth Symphony, extinguishing all that is noble in it and unduly accentuating the loud and what you probably call the 'dynamic' passages. But, sir, the Ninth is the symphony of brotherly love, mind you. . . . How can one conduct such an appeal to mankind and remain a Nazi?"

In the spring of 1938, the Nazi battalions moved into Austria. When Toscanini heard the news that Seyss-Inquart, the pro-Nazi, had entered the Austrian cabinet—the first straw in the wind that *Anschluss* was at hand—Toscanini burst into tears. He had been happy conducting in Salzburg. But he also knew the position he would have to take. On February 17, 1938, he cabled to the directors of the Salzburg Festival that he could not participate there any longer. Nor anywhere else, where Nazis would penetrate. . . .

Meanwhile, Toscanini had made still another gesture of defiance to the Nazis, and another gesture of sympathy and help to the oppressed of the world.

Many of the great Jewish musical artists who had been driven out of Germany had found refuge in Palestine. In 1935, the celebrated concert violinist, Bronislaw Huberman, conceived the project of gathering these musicians into a new orchestra. Thus the Palestine Symphony came into being, composed of some of Germany's one-time finest orchestral musicians. To give the orchestra immediate artistic significance—and to draw to it the attention of the world— Huberman asked Toscanini to conduct the inaugural concert in Tel-Aviv.

Toscanini did not have to be asked twice. It was his duty, he said, to show the entire world in the only way he could his sympathy with the Jewish people at a time when they were being barbarously persecuted. Though not too well, he flew to Tel-Aviv in December of 1936 to begin rehearsals. Not only did he refuse any compensation for his performance, but he also insisted on paying his own traveling expenses! On December 26, the Palestine Symphony made its momentous bow under Toscanini. It was an important musical event, marking as it did the birth of one of the world's great orchestras, and the first of Toscanini's appearances in the Near East. But it was also an important *political* event—a testimony that oppression could be fought and that free men could triumph.

It was Toscanini the humanitarian, rather than Toscanini the musician, who was honored on May 27, 1947, with the "One World Award for Music"—in recognition of his "outstanding achievements in the resistance to oppression and for the advancement of freedom."

9.   The N. B. C. Symphony

THE season of 1935-1936 was Toscanini's last with
the New York Philharmonic. The taxing schedule
calling for four concerts a week was too much for one who
made such formidable demands on himself. Toscanini was
tired and overwrought. Regretfully, the directors of the
Philharmonic accepted his resignation, only too conscious
of what they were losing.

Toscanini's last Philharmonic concert on April 29, 1936,
was overwhelming proof of how much he had come to
mean to the concert audiences of New York. Aware that
they may perhaps be hearing him for the last time, the
city's music lovers formed a queue to the box office ten
hours before concert time for the standing-room tickets
that would be put on sale an hour before performance.
Seats had long been sold out. And when the concert ended

with Wagner's *The Ride of the Valkyries*, the demonstration given Toscanini was one of the most moving witnessed in Carnegie Hall. With tumult and shouting New York was bidding farewell to its best-loved musician.

But Toscanini was not permanently lost to New York as was first believed to be the case on that April evening. Many musicians considered the absence of Toscanini from the American concert scene an intolerable situation calling for remedy, but there was not much they could do. But there was someone who felt he could do something. He was David Sarnoff, head of the Radio Corporation of America, who had at his disposal the facilities and resources of both the National Broadcasting Company and RCA Victor Records. He called Samuel Chotzinoff, then the music critic of the New York *Post*, an intimate friend of Toscanini, to inquire if there was any way in which the National Broadcasting Company could bring Toscanini back to America. Sarnoff pointed out that Toscanini, conducting for the National Broadcasting Company, could be heard not only by a visible audience of several thousand, but also by many millions, through the facilities of the largest radio network available to the Company. Thus the acquisition of Toscanini would not only be a *coup* for the N.B.C., but it would also be one for American music as well.

Chotzinoff doubted seriously if Toscanini would be amenable to conducting for radio. But the effort of getting him was worth making. With his wife, Chotzinoff set sail for Europe to visit the Toscaninis at their Milan home on Via Durini. It was to Mrs. Toscanini that Chotzinoff first unfolded the plan. Mrs. Toscanini had long felt that the art of her husband, now at its greatest, should be heard by audiences far greater than those that can fill an auditorium. She was sympathetic to the project and was confident that Toscanini would be, too. With Mrs. Toscanini as a formidable ally, Chotzinoff set out to break down Toscanini's resistance.

"Maestro, have you heard of the National Broadcasting Company?" Chotzinoff asked cautiously.

The Maestro had heard of it vaguely.

"Have you heard of David Sarnoff?" Chotzinoff continued.

Toscanini shook his head, no.

Chotzinoff came straight to the point: "Well, they both want you to come back to America."

Carefully and meticulously Chotzinoff outlined to Toscanini the entire project. The National Broadcasting Company was willing to organize a new symphony orchestra for Toscanini, the best possible. The orchestra would perform a weekly concert for most of the year under leading conductors. For a given period, Toscanini would take over. The orchestra would perform in a specially constructed studio for a living audience of several thousand; at the same time, the concert would be broadcast throughout the United States and Canada over the complete N.B.C. network.

"I will come," Toscanini said simply.

It had been as easy as all that! It took Chotzinoff several moments to realize that he had succeeded in his mission, and with almost childish ease. He leaped to the telephone to call David Sarnoff in New York with the momentous news.

The details were easily attended to. Toscanini was to

direct ten concerts during the first season, and was to receive one of the highest fees ever paid a conductor: $4,000 a concert, with N.B.C. paying Toscanini's taxes to the government. The wheels would be set into motion for the creation of a new great symphony orchestra.

The entire country was combed for the finest instrumentalists that could be found. For weeks the process of elimination and refinement took place until only the finest material remained. Then Artur Rodzinski (then the conductor of the Cleveland Orchestra) was called to whip the orchestra into shape. Famous as one of the best organizers among conductors, Rodzinski spent four intense weeks of rehearsals, welding together the disparate parts of the orchestra into a unified whole. On the evening of November 13, 1937, the N.B.C. Symphony Orchestra made its bow, Pierre Monteux conducting. That concert proved how well Rodzinski had succeeded in preparing the orchestra for its debut. The N.B.C. Symphony sounded that night as if it had been many years in existence. Two more concerts conducted by Monteux, and three by Rodzinski— and the orchestra was ready for its distinguished musical director.

On Christmas evening, Toscanini returned to American music by directing the N.B.C. Symphony in a program that included the G minor Symphony of Mozart and the First Symphony of Brahms. It had cost the National Broadcasting Company close to $250,000 to bring Toscanini back to the American people. An audience estimated at 20,000,000 listened—the largest audience ever to hear a concert.

At the conclusion of that first season, David Sarnoff announced that Toscanini had consented to return to the

N.B.C. Symphony for two additional years. Actually, Toscanini was to return for many years more than that, bringing his incomparable music to a fabulous-sized audience, not only by means of the radio, but also through phonograph records. In the strictest sense, Toscanini now belonged to all America.

During the Pan-American Conference, held in Lima in 1938, it was suggested that a tour of the N.B.C. Symphony under Toscanini might be a powerful force for cementing good relations between the United States and South America. The suggestion struck a responsive chord both with the American State Department and with the executives of the National Broadcasting Company. Toscanini was also very much in favor of it. He had always had a warm feeling for South America, where he had made his momentous debut so many years ago. And since it was more than two decades that he had last appeared there, he was eager to return.

But it took close to two years to realize the project. On June 1, a large contingent of the N.B.C. Symphony, Toscanini, Samuel Chotzinoff, and the N.B.C. executive, John F. Royal, set sail on the *Brazil*.

Toscanini and the N.B.C. Symphony gave sixteen concerts in three different South American countries, the first and the last taking place at Rio de Janeiro on June 12 and July 10 respectively. It is doubtful that any musician in South America ever received such an overwhelming ovation as Toscanini did during this tour. It was, as Samuel Chotzinoff told an interviewer, ". . . absolutely terrific. At Montevideo, there was such enthusiasm that the crowds, after several encores, still whistled and stamped. It threatened to tear the house down unless the maestro came out again, which he did. After his first concert in Rio de Janeiro there was virtually a stampede in the auditorium. I have never seen such audiences."

It is an interesting commentary on the political currents of the time that the Italian and German embassies in South America tried to use their far-flung influence to have the Toscanini concerts boycotted. By letter, telephone, and wire they urged all South Americans of Italian or German extraction to stay away. If this gesture had an effect it was certainly not apparent at the box office where tickets, priced between $9.00 and $50.00 each, were simply not enough to meet the demand. For hours people stood in line to try to hear the concerts. Failing to get in, they thronged outside of Toscanini's hotel for an opportunity of seeing him even briefly. Toscanini was so besieged by such idolatrous mobs wherever he went that military guards had to be used to protect him.

The tour over, Toscanini sent a personal farewell note to each of his musicians a few hours before the ship docked in New York. "You have never played so well, so inspired," it read. "We have never been so linked before. We must be proud of what we have done. While writing, I feel sad at heart, and it will always be so when beautiful things come to an end."

The forces of nazism and fascism were now at war with the free people of the world.

Toscanini, who had fought them so bitterly up to now, joined the war effort. He conducted numerous concerts

over the radio and in auditoriums for war benefits—the
Red Cross, U.S.O., War Bonds, etc.—consistently refusing
payment for his services. He even compromised with his
savage artistic conscience by conducting radio programs of
lighter classics for the armed forces overseas, since he felt
that the fighting men wanted lighter fare in their musical
entertainment. At each one of his concerts he played *The
Star-Spangled Banner* as though its performance were some
sort of dedication: He looked upon the anthem as the
musical symbol for the freedom for which the United Nations were fighting.

For years, Hollywood had made truly fabulous offers to
him to appear in, or perform for, the motion pictures. He
turned them down unhesitatingly. The inevitable glorifica-
tion of his personality in which the cinema would have
indulged was repugnant to him. Besides, he would not
subject his hypersensitive eyes to the torture of Klieg lights.
Yet when the Office of War Information asked him to
appear in, and conduct for, a propaganda film to be distributed throughout the world, his answer was quick and
positive. He performed Verdi's *Hymn of Nations*, prefaced
by a brief camera glimpse at his home life. By rewriting one
of the lines of the text to include the phrase "Italy—
Betrayed!" and by interpolating into the score the anthems
of the United Nations, he created a powerful propaganda
vehicle for the war effort.

Surely it is eloquent poetic justice that the first radio
announcement of Mussolini's resignation should interrupt
a Toscanini concert. This happened on July 25, 1943, while
Toscanini directed a Verdi program over N.B.C. What the

news of Mussolini's downfall meant to Toscanini—who
had been one of the first to fight against his dictatorship,
and one of the most consistent in his opposition—can only
be imagined. He wept for joy, not for himself, but for all
the Italian people who, at long last, shook themselves loose
of tyranny. "At last, at last," he exclaimed, "my country
is saved." A few weeks after this event, the Italian army
surrendered to the forces of the United Nations. To commemorate this, Toscanini directed a special radio concert.
He called it "Victory Concert—Act I." The second and
third acts would come on V-E and V-J days.

Back in 1938 Toscanini had made a personal vow that
he would not return to his country as long as fascism ruled
there. But now fascism had been overthrown. Mussolini,
its architect, had been killed by an aroused people. Italy
was free again. A free Italy called to Toscanini to return.
For a while, there was a movement to make Toscanini the
first president of liberated Italy, just as another great musician, Paderewski, had been first president of a liberated
Poland after World War I. But Toscanini would not consider politics. As an alternative, Italy asked him to return
and conduct at La Scala. La Scala, which had been razed
to the ground by Allied bombs, had been partially restored.
Would Toscanini conduct a concert in honor of the re-
opening of the theater—*his* theater?

Toscanini, of course, accepted—refusing any payment
or traveling expenses. In Milan, he eagerly inspected the
rebuilt La Scala, clapped his hands to test the acoustics.
"It is the same," he exclaimed. He entered upon rehearsals
with a nervousness he rarely before betrayed. On this mo-

mentous occasion—his return to his native land after an absence of eight years—he wanted to be at his very best.

That return to the land of his birth—and to La Scala, the scene of some of his greatest triumphs—was surely as moving an episode as can be found in the music of our generation. The great and the humble swarmed to La Scala on the evening of May 11, 1946, not so much to hear great music, as to pay homage to the noblest Italian of them all. Everyone who could buy a ticket was inside the theater; some had paid as much as $200. Those who could not afford the price, crowded outside the opera house to hear the concert from loud speakers.

And then, as a correspondent for *The New York Times*, cabled:

"At one minute before nine o'clock, silence fell on the audience, the expectation became almost visible, and finally a small figure, well known to many in the house, appeared from the wings. As the first wave of applause broke loose, the maestro, head a little bent, the crown of his white hair sparkling in the innumerable lights, strode briskly to the podium. The applause became more intense. Then the audience rose and shouted its welcome, mingling in the acclaim the two names dearest to its heart—Toscanini and Italia. Many eyes, and no doubt Toscanini's eyes, too, were dimmed with tears."

Toscanini led ten concerts at La Scala, which brought in $120,000 to a fund for completion of the opera house's rehabilitation. After his final concert on the evening of June 26—he played Beethoven's Ninth Symphony—the audience yelled at him: *"Ritorno presto, ritorno maestro!* Come back quickly, maestro!"

Toscanini was to return to Italy frequently after that, sometimes for vacation, sometimes to conduct special performances. But to return to Italy permanently, to re-establish his home in his native land, no longer entered his thoughts.

His long stay in America, since 1938, had transformed him into an American. He could no longer live happily, nor function to his fullest capacities, anywhere else. His proud democratic spirit responded sympathetically to the American ideal; his personality and temperament found continual delight in the American way of life. Characteristically, he began more and more to adopt the enthusiasms and interests of Americans: Mickey Mouse films; jam sessions; prize fights. Characteristically, too, he began conducting (for the first time in his career) such authentically American works as Gershwin's *Rhapsody in Blue*, Grofe's *Grand Canyon Suite*, Gould's *A Lincoln Legend*, Siegmeister's *Western Suite*. He conducted this music now for the same reason that he began assimilating American interests: he was sensitively attuned to the country, and felt himself a part of it.

His increasing identification with the land of his adoption stimulated Toscanini's curiosity in America's geography, people, customs, backgrounds. This curiosity, in turn, awakened a new ambition. He wanted to come more personally into contact with the country in all its variety, to tour it extensively, to visit places he had read or heard about but had never seen. He wanted to conduct living concerts for Americans in their own communities.

The executives of the National Broadcasting Company and RCA Victor Records stood ready to satisfy this ambition. They provided the sponsorship for a nation-wide tour. A few days after the itinerary had been announced, tickets for the Toscanini concerts were completely sold out in most cities.

On April 17, 1950, the Toscanini train moved out of Pennsylvania Station in New York City, to begin a journey that was to cover 8,593 miles and embrace twenty cities. The twelve cars of the train proved to be a mighty caravan: Toscanini's private suite (a veritable hotel on wheels); a pressroom for reporters and press representatives; a library of 3,108 musical scores; a repository for $250,000 worth of musical instruments; extra lounge and dining and sleeping cars for the 110 men of the orchestra and the additional personnel required to take care of the many details of the tour; a larder stocked with enough food to provide approximately 1,000 meals a day.

The first stop was Baltimore, Maryland. The tour then progressed southward through Richmond and Atlanta; veered westward all the way to California; went north to Oregon and the state of Washington; finally reverted east to be concluded with a concert at Washington, D. C., before an audience including President Truman and most of the leading Government and diplomatic officials.

Few musical events in American music were looked forward to with such feverish anticipation; few were received with such enthusiasm and excitement. To most of those who came to hear him, Toscanini was a legend coming to life—a man who was now stepping out of fables, legends, and musical history into vibrant reality. The audiences came from a radius of several hundred miles, many in trains and buses specially chartered from distant places. Not even torrential rains in Dallas, Texas, could keep them away; indeed, several hundred, who did not have tickets, braved the storm and stood in the rain, drenched to the skin, with the elusive hope that somehow, in some way, they might be able to hear the concert. After each performance, the enthusiasm reached monumental proportions; ovation followed ovation in seemingly interminable waves of excited appreciation.

The trials, fatigues, nervous debilitation of such a tour sapped the vitality of everyone connected with it. Only Toscanini—eighty-three years young!—seemed able to take it all in his stride. He enjoyed every minute of it. Despite the enervation of almost continual travel, the fatigue of regular rehearsals, the physical and nervous exhaustion of conducting twenty-one concerts, the strain of the pressing social demands continually made on him, Toscanini always appeared in good spirits, fresh, indefatigable. He found the time and strength to do considerable sightseeing and to meet personally a great many people. He went to hear jazz in its birthplace in New Orleans, studied the colonial architecture of Williamsburg, Virginia, took excursions in Texas and Oregon, gleefully rode up a ski-tow in Sun Valley, Idaho. Then with a full and active day and evening behind him, he would sit up half the night talking over his experiences and impressions with friends. He brought an insatiable curiosity to everything he heard and saw. To everything happening to him he reacted with almost childlike fascination and wonder.

Toscanini had discovered America and the American people. It was partly to express his closeness to both that he conducted such typically American numbers as *Dixie* and Sousa's *The Stars and Stripes Forever.* (Senator Harry F. Byrd of Virginia had recorded the playing of *Dixie* by Toscanini in *The Congressional Record.*) Even before the tour ended, he spoke of undertaking others, equally extensive, to cities and communities that had not been on his itinerary.

Back in New York, Toscanini gave a lawn party for his orchestra at his home in Riverdale. It was an expression of gratitude for their co-operation in having made his tour— as he took special pains to point out to them—the happiest and the most memorable he had ever undertaken.

10. The Other Toscanini

TOSCANINI likes to say: "There are two Toscaninis, and only one of them is a bad man."

He is not proud of the demoniac passions that seize him when he is rehearsing. After his fury has been released and has been spent, he appears as flustered as a boy caught in an act of mischief. He becomes extravagantly penitent and humble, is often effusive in his apologies, and full of meek promises that never again will he lose control of himself. And, perhaps at the very next rehearsal, all good intentions are dissipated by an inadequate performance, and the old paroxysms return. He cannot help himself. An Italian psychiatrist once explained why. This happened in 1919 when Toscanini was sued in the Italian courts for assault and battery by a violinist whom Toscanini had attacked with his baton during rehearsal. The psychiatrist explained (and his explanation helped to absolve Toscanini): "He becomes transfigured by genius. . . . In a paroxysm of inspiration he falls prey to the tyranny of art."

But the "other Toscanini"—the Toscanini released from the tensions of making music—is usually gentle, warm-hearted, sympathetic, and sentimental. No one knows this better than the musicians themselves, the same men whom he abuses so ruthlessly during working hours. There are some conductors who snobbishly prefer to keep themselves at all times at a distance from their men, and have no per-onal interest in them whatsoever. Toscanini is certainly ot one of them. He feels very close to, and is always concerned with, each one of his musicians. He was happy at receiving a gold lifetime honorary membership card in Local 802 of the American Federation of Musicians because it officially made him one of them. He likes having his men drop in on him before rehearsals to chat and exchange light banter (which they feel free to do). And he enjoys being a host at parties which, at periodic intervals, he arranges for them and at which he is the last word in graciousness, personally concerned that everybody is being taken care of with food and drink.

The bond that ties him to his men is particularly evident when he tours with them. While traveling, he assumes a kind of paternal solicitude. The men of the New York Philharmonic still tell of the time when one of them fell seriously ill, when orchestra and conductor crossed the Atlantic en route to Europe. Toscanini stayed vigilantly at the man's bedside until he recovered. When Toscanini toured South America with the N.B.C. Symphony, he continually betrayed his sympathy and thoughtfulness. In

Montevideo, on the morning of July 4, he hurriedly assembled the orchestra for a brief rehearsal. "I'm not going to work you today," he said simply. "But today is your Independence Day, and you are all far from home. I thought you might like to play *The Star-Spangled Banner*." On the same tour, while the orchestra was in Rio de Janeiro for its final concert, the violist Jacques Tuschinsky was killed by a bus. The news was withheld from Toscanini until the voyage home. When he heard it he was inconsolable, wept like a child, refused to eat, kept himself aloof in his stateroom. When he recovered from this genuine grief he raised a subscription for the musician's widow to which he himself contributed $1,000.

During the 1950 tour of the United States, Toscanini once again became the father of a large brood. From time to time he would leave his private car to visit the men and see how they were getting along. On days off, as in Sun Valley, he mingled with them in genuine good fellowship. When the orchestra, in a spirit of fun, started playing parodies of Wagner and Sousa, Toscanini immediately entered into the spirit of the thing. He got up and began conducting them in mock seriousness.

The "other Toscanini" is known also to his relatives and intimate friends. In the concert auditorium, his may be an Olympian stature. But in the privacy of his own home, surrounded by those he loves, he is unaffectedly simple and humble. You will never find Toscanini putting on airs of grandeur or temperament. Being of Latin blood, he may at times have an explosive temper or indulge in volatile moods. But that is not the rule. Most often he is gay and easy to get along with, a most charming and considerate companion, and a most devoted grandfather, father, and husband.

His simplicity reveals itself in many different ways. He derives inordinate pleasure from such comparatively little things as playing pranks on friends and relatives (he grows as furious as a spoiled child when they don't quite come off!), strolling in his garden, toying with gadgets. In the last few years he has become a television addict; and, through television, he has become a rabid prize-fight fan. He knows some of the fine points of the science. When a fight reaches a climax he is not only an observant but participant as well. He jumps out of his seat, emulates the proceedings on the television in a display of shadowboxing, shrieking all the time at the top of his voice, "Keel heem! Keel heem!"

He never smokes, rarely drinks anything stronger than wine (and that sparingly) and has never had much interest in games of chance. His taste in food is almost modest, a carry-over no doubt from his boyhood days when he had so little to eat. He usually partakes of thick soup and bread at his principal meal, and at other times nibbles at fruit or cheese. His dress has also been just as modest, though always in good taste. He is not conscious of how much money he has, or how much he is earning; all his life he has been sublimely disinterested in acquiring wealth. When he is negotiating with people who can afford to pay well for his services, he can drive a hard bargain. But, as his biography has proved again and again, he is the most generous of musicians in donating his services—and often even large sums of money—for notable causes.

As a musician he may flee from applause and honors and adulation and the madding throng. But away from music he is not a man to enjoy solitude. Villa Pauline (his eight-acre, twenty-one room estate in Riverdale, at the outskirts of New York City) usually swarms with visitors because he likes to have them around him. When he cannot have his friends near him at his own home he goes out visiting. He wants to have his immediate family near at hand at all times, and is happiest when they are all assembled around him. His wife, Carla, was a dancer when she married him in 1897. They have three children, Walter is now Toscanini's business manager. Wanda is married to the world-famous pianist, Vladimir Horowitz. Another daughter, Wally, has been the Countess Castelbarco. There was a fourth child, Giorgio, who died when he was eight years old.

If he has any passions, it is for staying up late at night, surrounded by his friends, and participating in stimulating conversation on art and politics. Since he requires very little sleep—four or five hours suffice—he can indulge this whim without affecting his health. And regardless of how late he goes to sleep, he is always up at about six in the morning, usually awakening his whole family with his high-pitched singing as he dresses. His culture is expansive. His reservoir of information is overflowing, his memory of things read fabulous. Novelists, scientists, statesmen have often been impressed by the flexible range of his intellect. But in the company of those he likes he can be not only a brilliant conversationalist, but also a vivacious companion who enjoys indulgence in a whimsical kind of humor. Once when a nearby radio was broadcasting a symphony concert conducted by Stokowski, Toscanini suddenly fell on his knees in full view of his startled guests, clasped his hands in prayer and begged: "Please, Mr. Stokowski, no more *ritenuti*, no more *ritenuti!*" He is perhaps at his most charming in the society of young people. Somehow he likes to think of himself as one of them. At one of his parties, long after midnight, he whispered to a few youngsters near him: "Soon the old folk will go home. Then *we* will have real fun!"

The night has not necessarily ended for Toscanini when the last guest has gone. He usually finds time now for reading in bed. He has always been a voracious reader, his poor eyesight notwithstanding. In classic literature he admires most Dante, Goethe, Shelley, and Shakespeare. He originally learned English many years ago in order to read Shelley and Shakespeare in the original. He has read everything Shakespeare has written, and much of it he has committed to memory. In contemporary writing, he prefers biographies, essays, and histories to fiction.

Sometimes he will open a score by Beethoven—a score which he may have conducted hundreds of times and of which he surely knows every note. He reads it through, from first page to last, as if it were a new work. "Now that I am old," he once told a friend, "I want to come closer to the secrets of Beethoven."

Appendixes

1
MILESTONES IN TOSCANINI'S CAREER

2
SOME IMPORTANT WORLD PREMIERES CONDUCTED BY TOSCANINI

3
FOR FURTHER READING ON TOSCANINI

4
A COMPLETE LIST OF TOSCANINI RECORDINGS

Appendix 1

MILESTONES IN TOSCANINI'S CAREER

March 25, 1867   Born in Parma, Italy

July 24, 1885   Graduates from the Parma Conservatory

June 26, 1886   Makes debut as conductor (in Rio de Janeiro, in Aïda)

November 4, 1886   Makes debut as conductor in Italy (in Turin, in Edmea)

March 1892   Conducts a Wagnerian opera for the first time (The Flying Dutchman)

May 2, 1892   Conducts world première of Leoncavallo's Pagliacci (in Milan)

February 1, 1896   Conducts world première of Puccini's La Bohème (in Turin)

December 26, 1898   Conducts first opera performance at La Scala in Milan (Die Meistersinger)

November 16, 1908   Conducts first performance at the Metropolitan Opera House in New York (Aïda)

December 10, 1910   Conducts world première of Puccini's *The Girl of the Golden West* (in New York)

December 28, 1920   Conducts first concert in American tour with the La Scala Orchestra (in New York)

December 6, 1921   Returns to La Scala as artistic director (*Falstaff*)

January 14, 1926   Conducts first concert with the New York Philharmonic Orchestra

April 25, 1926   Conducts world première of Puccini's *Turandot* (in Milan)

May 3, 1930   Directs first concert of European tour with the New York Philharmonic (in Paris)

July 22, 1930   Conducts for the first time at Bayreuth (*Tannhäuser*)

August 23, 1934   Conducts for the first time at the Salzburg Festival (orchestral concert)

December 26, 1936   Conducts concert with which the Palestine Symphony Orchestra is founded (Tel-Aviv)

December 25, 1937   Conducts first concert with the NBC Symphony

June 12, 1940   Conducts first concert of South American tour with NBC Symphony (in Rio de Janeiro)

May 11, 1946   Conducts first concert in Italy in fifteen years (at La Scala in Milan)

April 18, 1950   Conducts first concert of American tour with NBC Symphony (in Baltimore, Md.)

Appendix 2

SOME IMPORTANT WORLD PREMIERES CONDUCTED BY TOSCANINI

(Arranged Chronologically)

May 21, 1892: *Pagliacci*, by Ruggiero Leoncavallo (Milan)

February 1, 1896: *La Bohème*, by Giacomo Puccini (Turin)

November 10, 1900: *Zaza*, by Ruggiero Leoncavallo (Milan)

January 17, 1901: *Le Maschere*, by Pietro Mascagni (Milan)

November 16, 1901: *Mosè*, by Don Lorenzo Perosi (Milan)

March 11, 1902: *Germania*, by Alberto Franchetti (Milan)

April 15, 1907: *Gloria*, by Francesco Cilèa (Milan)

Spring, 1907: *Le Baruffe Chiozzotte*, overture, by Leone Sinigaglia (Milan)

December 10, 1910: *The Girl of the Golden West*, by Giacomo Puccini (New York)

January 25, 1915: *Madame Sans-Gêne*, by Umberto Giordano (New York)

122   *Story of Arturo Toscanini*

November 16, 1916: *Chiari di Luna*, by Vincenzo Tommasini (Rome)

January 27, 1918: *Pause del Silenzio*, by Gian Francesco Malipiero (Rome)

December 16, 1922: *Débora e Jaéle*, by Ildebrando Pizzetti (Milan)

May 1, 1924: *Nerone*, by Arrigo Boïto (Milan)

December 20, 1924: *La Cena delle Beffe*, by Umberto Giordano (Milan)

March 7, 1925: *I Cavalieri di Ekebù*, by Riccardo Zandonai (Milan)

January 21, 1926: *Gethsemani*, by Victor de Sabata (Milan)

April 25, 1926: *Turandot*, by Giacomo Puccini (Milan)

March 15, 1928: *Rondo Arlecchinesco*, by Ferruccio Busoni (New York)

May 16, 1928: *Fra Gherardo*, by Ildebrando Pizzetti (Milan)

January 10, 1929: *Il Re*, by Umberto Giordano (Milan)

February 21, 1929: *Feste Romane*, by Ottorino Respighi (New York)

February 28, 1929: *Concerto dell' Estate*, by Ildebrando Pizzetti (New York)

October 10, 1929: *El Carnevale di Venezia*, by Vincenzo Tommasini (New York)

February 27, 1930: *Rondo Veneziano*, by Ildebrando Pizzetti (New York)

April 3, 1930: *Summer Evening*, by Zoltán Kodály (New York)

December 11, 1930: *Dances of Marosszék*, by Zoltán Kodály (New York)

April 6, 1931: *Introduction to Agamemnon*, by Ildebrando Pizzetti (New York)

April 8, 1931: *Flirtation in a Chinese Garden*, and *Parade*, by Abram Chasins (New York)

November 10, 1932: Symphony No. 2, by Bernard Wagenaar (New York)

April 12, 1933: Concerto No. 2, for violin and orchestra, by

Mario Castelnuovo-Tedesco, Jascha Heifetz soloist (New York)

January 31, 1935: Concerto for Cello and Orchestra, by Mario Castelnuovo-Tedesco, Gregor Piatigorsky soloist (New York)

November 25, 1938: *Adagio for Strings*, and *Essay No. 1*, by Samuel Barber (New York)

November 2, 1942: *A Lincoln Legend*, by Morton Gould (New York)

November 25, 1945: *A Midsummer Night's Dream Overture*, by Mario Castelnuovo-Tedesco (New York)

November 25, 1945: *Western Suite*, by Elie Siegmeister (New York)

(Arranged by composers)

Barber, Samuel: *Adagio for Strings*, and *Essay No. 1*

Boïto, Arrigo: *Nerone*

Busoni, Ferruccio: *Rondo Arlecchinesco*

Castelnuovo-Tedesco, Mario: Concerto for Cello and Orchestra, Concerto No. 2, for violin and orchestra, and *A Midsummer Night's Dream Overture*

Chasins, Abram: *Flirtation in a Chinese Garden*, and *Parade*

Cilèa, Francesco: *Gloria*

Franchetti, Alberto: *Germania*

Giordano, Umberto: *La Cena delle Beffe*, *Madame Sans-Gêne*, and *Il Re*

Gould, Morton: *A Lincoln Legend*

Kodály, Zoltán: *Dances of Marosszék*, and *Summer Evening*

Leoncavallo, Ruggiero: *Pagliacci*, and *Zaza*

Malipiero, Gian Francesco: *Pause del Silenzio*

Mascagni, Pietro: *Le Maschere*

Perosi, Don Lorenzo: *Mosè*

Pizzetti, Ildebrando: *Concerto dell' Estate*, *Débora e Jaéle*, *Fra Gherardo*, *Introduction to Agamemnon*, and *Rondo Veneziano*

Puccini, Giacomo: *La Bohème, The Girl of the Golden West,* and *Turandot*

Respighi, Ottorino: *Feste Romane*

de Sabata, Victor: *Gethsemani*

Siegmeister, Elie: *Western Suite*

Sinigaglia, Leone: *Le Baruffe Chiozzotte,* overture

Tommasini, Vincenzo: *El Carnevale di Venezia,* and *Chiari di Luna*

Wagenaar, Bernard: *Symphony No. 2*

Zandonai, Riccardo: *I Cavalieri di Ekebù*

Appendix 3

FOR FURTHER READING ON TOSCANINI

(Books)

Ewen, David. *Dictators of the Baton* (revised edition). New York: Prentice-Hall, Inc., 1948.

Gilman, Lawrence. *Toscanini and Great Music*. New York: Farrar & Rinehart, 1938.

Hoeller, Susanne. *Arturo Toscanini: A Photobiography*. New York: Island Press, 1943.

O'Connell, Charles. *The Other Side of the Record*. New York: Alfred A. Knopf, Inc., 1947.

Sargeant, Winthrop. *Geniuses, Goddesses, and People*. New York: E. P. Dutton & Co., Inc., 1949.

Stefan, Paul. *Toscanini*. New York: The Viking Press, 1936.

Taubman, Howard: *Music on My Beat*. New York: Simon and Schuster, Inc., 1943.

(Magazine Articles)

Bronson, Arthur. "Toscanini," *The American Mercury*, November 1944.

Lingg, Ann M. "Toscanini," *Readers Digest*, August 1947.

Segre, Alfredo. "Toscanini: The First Forty Years," *Musical Quarterly*, April 1947.

Taubman, Howard. "Maestro," *Atlantic Monthly*, October 1947.

———. "Toscanini in America," *Musical Quarterly*, April 1947.

(Unsigned.) "The Perfectionist," *Time*, April 26, 1948.

Appendix 4

A COMPLETE LIST OF TOSCANINI RECORDINGS

Toscanini has recorded exclusively for RCA Victor.

All the listings below are available on the conventional 78 RPM records; many can be had on either 45 RPM records, or 33⅓ RPM records, or both. Since the transfer of the old conventional records to the newer speeds is continuing all the time, it is advisable for the reader to consult his local dealer if the Toscanini record he desires is available in the speed he prefers.

BARBER

    Adagio for Strings. NBC Symphony Orchestra. 78 RPM 11-8287.

BEETHOVEN

    Beethoven and Paganini Encores. (3 Selections.) NBC Symphony Orchestra. 78 RPM DM-590.

Concerto for Piano and Orchestra, No. 1, in C, Opus 15; Ania Dorfmann, Pianist; NBC Symphony Orchestra. 78 RPM DM-1036—45 RPM WDM-1036—33⅓ RPM LM-1039.

Concerto for Piano and Orchestra, No. 3, in C Minor, Opus 37; Artur Rubinstein, Pianist; NBC Symphony Orchestra. 78 RPM DM-1016.

Concerto for Violin and Orchestra, in D, Opus 61; Jascha Heifetz, Violinist; NBC Symphony Orchestra. 78 RPM DM-705.

Coriolan Overture, Opus 62. NBC Symphony Orchestra. 78 RPM 11-9023—45 RPM 49-1176.

Fidelio: Abscheulicher, Wo Eilst du Hin? Rose Bampton, Soprano; NBC Symphony Orchestra. 78 RPM 11-9110.

Leonore Overture No. 1, in C, Opus 138. BBC Symphony Orchestra. 78 RPM 15945.

Leonore Overture No. 3, Opus 72a. NBC Symphony Orchestra. 78 RPM DM-1098—45 RPM WDM-1098—33⅓ RPM LM-1043 (reverse side: Daphnis and Chloe Suite No. 2, Ravel).

Overture to Consecration of the House, in C, Opus 124. NBC Symphony Orchestra. 78 RPM DM-1287—45 RPM WDM-1287—33⅓ RPM LM-6.

Symphony No. 1, in C, Opus 21. BBC Symphony Orchestra. 78 RPM DM-507.

Symphony No. 3, in E-Flat, Opus 55 ("Eroica"). NBC Symphony Orchestra. 78 RPM DM-1375—45 RPM WDM-1375 —33⅓ RPM LM-1042.

Symphony No. 3, in E-Flat, Opus 55 ("Eroica"). NBC Symphony Orchestra. 78 RPM DM-765.

Symphony No. 5, in C Minor, Opus 67. NBC Symphony Orchestra. 78 RPM DM-640.

Symphony No. 7, in A, Opus 92. Philharmonic-Symphony Orchestra of New York. 78 RPM DM-317.

Symphony No. 8, in F, Opus 93. NBC Symphony Orchestra. 78 RPM DM-908.

BERLIOZ

Roméo et Juliette, Opus 17 (Part II Excerpts). NBC Symphony Orchestra. 78 RPM DM-1160—45 RPM WDM-1160—33⅓ RPM LM-1019 (reverse side: Romeo and Juliet Overture, Tchaikovsky).

BRAHMS

Concerto for Piano and Orchestra, No. 2, in B-Flat, Opus 83; Vladimir Horowitz, Pianist; NBC Symphony Orchestra. 78 RPM DM-740.
Symphony No. 1, in C Minor, Opus 68. NBC Symphony Orchestra. 78 RPM DM-875.
Tragic Overture, Opus 81. BBC Symphony Orchestra. 78 RPM DM-507.
Variations on a Theme by Haydn, Opus 56a. Philharmonic-Symphony Orchestra of New York. 78 RPM DM-355.

DUKAS

Sorcerer's Apprentice, The. Philharmonic-Symphony Orchestra of New York. 78 RPM 7021.

GROFE

Grand Canyon Suite. NBC Symphony Orchestra. 78 RPM DM-1038—45 RPM WDM-1038—33⅓ RPM LM-1004.

HAYDN

Symphony No. 88, in G, Old B. and H. No. 13. NBC Symphony Orchestra. 78 RPM DM-454.
Symphony No. 98, in B-Flat. NBC Symphony Orchestra. 78 RPM DM-1025.
Symphony No. 101, in D ("Clock"). NBC Symphony Orchestra. 78 RPM DM-1368—45 RPM WDM-1368—33⅓ RPM LM-1038 (reverse side: Symphony No. 35, in D, K. 385 ["Haffner"], Mozart).

MENDELSSOHN

Midsummer Night's Dream, A (Incidental Music). NBC Symphony Orchestra; Edna Phillips, Soprano, and Women's Choral 78 RPM DM-1280.

MOZART

Concerto for Bassoon and Orchestra, No. 1, in B-Flat, K. 191; Leonard Sharrow, Bassoonist; NBC Symphony Orchestra. 78 RPM DM-1304—45 RPM WDM-1304—33⅓ RPM LM-1030 (reverse side: Symphony No. 41, in C, K. 551 ["Jupiter"], Mozart).

Divertimento for Strings and Two Horns, No. 15, in B-Flat, K. 287. NBC Symphony Orchestra. 78 RPM DM-1355—45 RPM WDM-1355—33⅓ RPM LM-13.

Magic Flute, The: Overture. BBC Symphony Orchestra. 78 RPM 15190—45 RPM 49-0903.

Symphony, No. 35, in D, K. 385 ("Haffner"). NBC Symphony Orchestra. 78 RPM DM-1172—45 RPM WDM-1172—33⅓RPM LM-1038 (reverse side: Symphony, No. 101, in D ["Clock"], Haydn)

Symphony, No. 40, in G Minor, K. 550. NBC Symphony Orchestra. 78 RPM DM-631.

Symphony, No. 41, in C, K. 551 ("Jupiter"). NBC Symphony Orchestra. 78 RPM DM-1080—45 RPM WDM-1080—33⅓ RPM LM-1030 (reverse side: Concerto for Bassoon and Orchestra, No. 1, in B-Flat, K. 191, Mozart).

PAGANINI

Beethoven and Paganini Encores. (3 Selections.) NBC Symphony Orchestra. 78 RPM DM-590.

RAVEL

Daphnis and Chloe Suite, No. 2. NBC Symphony Orchestra. 78 RPM DM-1374—45 RPM WDM-1374—33⅓ RPM LM-1043 (reverse side: Leonore Overture, No. 3, Opus 72a, Beethoven)

ROSSINI

Barber of Seville: Overture. Philharmonic-Symphony Orchestra of New York. 78 RPM 7255.

Italiana in Algeri, L': Overture. Philharmonic-Symphony Orchestra of New York. 78 RPM 14161.

Rossini Overtures. (5 Selections.) NBC Symphony Orchestra. 78 RPM DM-1037—45 RPM WDM-1037—33⅓ RPM LM-1044.

Scala di seta, La: Overture. BBC Symphony Orchestra. 78 RPM 15191.

Semiramide: Overture. Philharmonic-Symphony Orchestra of New York, 78 RPM DM-408.

Three Rossini Overtures. BBC Symphony Orchestra and Philharmonic-Symphony Orchestra of New York. 78 RPM DM-825.

William Tell: Overture. NBC Symphony Orchestra. 78 RPM DM-605—45 RPM WDM-605—33⅓ RPM LM-14 (reverse side: The Skaters Waltz, *Waldteufel*).

SCHUBERT

Symphony, No. 9, in C. NBC Symphony Orchestra. 78 RPM DM-1167—45 RPM WDM-1167—33⅓ RPM LM-1040.

SCHUMANN

Overture to Manfred, Opus 115. NBC Symphony Orchestra. 78 RPM DM-1287—45 RPM WDM-1287—33⅓ RPM LM-6.

SOUSA

Stars and Stripes Forever. NBC Symphony Orchestra. 78 RPM 11-9188.

STRAUSS, JOHANN, JR.

On the Beautiful Blue Danube—Waltz. NBC Symphony Orchestra. 78 RPM 11-8580.

Tritsch-Tratsch Polka. NBC Symphony Orchestra. 78 RPM 11-9188.

TCHAIKOVSKY

Concerto for Piano and Orchestra, No. 1, in B-Flat Minor, Opus 23; Vladimir Horowitz, Pianist; NBC Symphony Orchestra. 78 RPM DM-800.

Manfred, Opus 58 (Symphonic Poem). NBC Symphony Orchestra. 78 RPM DM-1372—45 RPM WDM-1372—33⅓ RPM LM-1037.

Romeo and Juliet Overture. NBC Symphony Orchestra. 78 RPM DM-1178—45 RPM WDM-1178—33⅓ RPM LM-1019 (reverse side: Roméo et Juliette, Opus 17 [Part II Excerpts], Berlioz).

Symphony No. 6, in B Minor, Opus 74 ("Pathétique"). NBC Symphony Orchestra. 78 RPM DM-1281—45 RPM WDM-1281—33⅓ RPM LM-1036.

THOMAS

Mignon: Overture. NBC Symphony Orchestra; Arthur Berv, Horn Soloist. 78 RPM 11-8545.

VERDI

⟩*Forza del destino, La: Overture.* NBC Symphony Orchestra. 78 RPM 11-9010.

Traviata, La: Preludes to Act I and Act III. NBC Symphony Orchestra. 78 RPM 18080.

WAGNER

Götterdämmerung, Die: Brunnhilde's Immolation; Helen Traubel, Soprano; NBC Symphony Orchestra. 78 RPM DM-978.

Götterdämmerung, Die: Siegfried's Rhine Journey and Funeral Music. NBC Symphony Orchestra. 78 RPM DM-853.

Lohengrin: Act I; Prelude. NBC Symphony Orchestra. 78 RPM 11-8807.

Meistersinger, Die: Prelude. NBC Symphony Orchestra. 78 RPM 11-9385—45 RPM 49-0297.

Parsifal: Prelude and Good Friday Spell. NBC Symphony Orchestra. 78 RPM DM-1376—45 RPM WDM-1376—33⅓ RPM LM-15.

Wagner Program, A. (3 Selections.) NBC Symphony Orchestra. 78 RPM DM-1135.

Wagnerian Excerpts. (5 Selections.) Philharmonic-Symphony Orchestra of New York. 78 RPM DM-308.

WALDTEUFEL

Skaters Waltz, The. NBC Symphony Orchestra. 78 RPM 11-8949—45 RPM 49-0132—33⅓ RPM LM-14 (reverse side: William Tell: Overture, *Rossini*).

WEBER

Freischütz, Der: Overture. NBC Symphony Orchestra. 78 RPM 11-9172.

Invitation to the Dance, Opus 65. BBC Symphony Orchestra. 78 RPM 15192.

Index

Index